Systems Thinking in the Public Se..... ....

Delivering Public Services that Work

Volume One

Edited by Peter Middleton

Foreword by John Seddon

Published in this first edition in 2010 by:
Triarchy Press
Station Offices
Axminster
Devon. EX13 5PF
United Kingdom

+44 (0)1297 631456
info@triarchypress.com
www.triarchypress.com

A catalogue record for this book is available from the British Library.

Cover design by Heather Fallows ~
www.whitespacegallery.org.uk

ISBN: 978-0-9562631-6-2

Contents

Foreword

John Seddon

It is now ten years since I first became involved with the public sector. At that time I was critical of central government's attempts at change but found public sector managers too fearful to heed my criticisms and advice; that same fear obliged them to comply, to do as directed, regardless.

Things have changed. Many public sector managers are actively rejecting bad and unproven directives. There are now more than a hundred public sector organisations employing systems thinking and the number of public sector people who know the counter-intuitive truths exposed by this knowledge must count in tens of thousands.

It is timely to publish these case studies. The profound improvements evidenced give an indication of the good that can be achieved across all public services. I anticipate that this will be the first of a series, for many readers will be curious about how the ideas might be applied to other public services.

All of the case studies have followed the Vanguard Method, the method I developed with colleagues, a means by which service organisations can learn to move away from a 'command-and-control' design and into a systems design. By normal standards this is an unusual approach to change. There are no cost-benefit analyses, no project plans and no predetermined 'deliverables'; instead the change starts with studying your service as a system. The consequence is thorough knowledge about the 'what and why' of current performance and thus confidence that the actions taken to re-design the service will lead to improvement. The improvements achieved are always greater than would have been thought achievable through conventional planning and change management.

This method also puts tools in their place. Tools are solutions to problems. The first thing you want to know is what problems you have, and studying your service as a system reveals that the problems you actually have are not the ones you think you have. When you know your problem(s) you can then find or fashion a tool. This is also the way Taiichi Ohno (the man who created the Toyota System) taught – studying the way services work as systems reveals the counter-intuitive truths, challenges to convention that are more easily understood and accepted if you see them for yourself.

Failing to understand your problems before determining solutions also explains why so many tools-based interventions fail. Tragically Ohno's brilliance has been packaged and promulgated as a set of 'lean' tools. I would suggest that if you are not in the business of producing cars at the rate of demand, the tools associated with solving the associated problems are unlikely to be of much help to you. Service organisations, as you will see, have different problems to solve and thus different tools to deploy or develop.

As public sector managers have set out to understand their organisations as systems they have learned how much of the centrally dictated requirements are part of the problem. While their natural fear of defying the centre has caused some to revert to what they know to be poor service designs, but which will attract good inspection reports, others have engaged in arguing with the centre. As the centre can't fire me I have been vociferous in my condemnation of many of the bad ideas promulgated, even coerced, into public services. In particular I have argued that the Audit Commission has been central to the dysfunctional regime.

My criticisms of the Audit Commission drew a riposte from one of its senior managers. He ignored the substantive issues and instead issued an ad-hominem attack. Amongst the eleven insults he said: 'Mr Seddon's clients will need to judge for themselves whether there is proof that his… nostrums work. They will take into account his own cavalier way with the evidence.'

You, the reader, must judge for yourself.

My thanks to the authors who have taken the time to write about their experiences and to Peter Middleton for taking these and editing them into a highly readable text.

John Seddon

OVERVIEW

The benefit you will obtain from this book is that you will gain insight into how to transform your organisation to achieve remarkable results.

This book presents evidence that there is a significantly better and cheaper way to manage public sector services than the present target driven approach. Systems thinking enables greatly improved services, lower costs and happier staff. It allows all but the most dysfunctional of government performance targets to be greatly exceeded.

The six case studies in this book will show you the way to achieve these results and give you examples. To obtain irrefutable proof you will need to experience the power of systems thinking for yourself. Allocate half a day and carry out the following free experiment:

1. Identify a service that you have access to. Preferably one that you perceive to be performing well.

2. Locate where this service interfaces with its customers. This is where customer phone calls, emails or visits are received. Listen to or observe 30 transactions. Write down, in their own words, <u>why</u> each customer contacted the organisation.

3. Write down how many of the contacts were unnecessary. Identify the 'failure demand' which would be preventable with better systems. E.g. how many of the contacts are from customers who were progress chasing or asking for help with complex forms or procedures? Work out what percentage of the total demand is 'failure demand'. This gives you a first indication of how much activity is preventable waste.

4. Take 10 of these customers and using the operation's records work out the total end-to-end elapsed time from when they first contacted the system to when they finally achieved their purpose. Note every interaction they had to go through. Phone them if possible to ensure you have recorded all the interactions. Put these 10 numbers into a graph to see how much they fluctuate.

5. Review the 'failure demand' and 'end-to-end time' data you have collected.

If you are disappointed or shocked by what you discover, read some of the books in the bibliography and try some more experiments. Your journey has begun!

What is Systems Thinking?

This book is made up of six case studies describing the application of systems thinking to management. Systems thinking emerged after the 2nd World War and several variants have since developed. The systems thinking method described here was created by John Seddon (Seddon, 2005, 2008) as a framework to enable organisations to achieve higher performance. It is unique in that it was developed by working in partnership with both private and public sector organisations for over two decades. It is therefore grounded in how organisations actually work and can be changed.

Due to the remarkable results it makes possible, this proprietary material has been placed in the public domain. It is the scale of waste that this method can make visible, and then show how to remove, that makes it too important to be kept private. An approach to management that enhances the quality of life of employees and customers, while reducing costs, just demands a wider audience.

This book is for managers, directors and board members of public sector organisations: particularly those who have to achieve targets or Key Performance Indicators (KPI) while having their budgets cut. The implementations of systems thinking described by your colleagues in this book will show you a way forward.

The purpose of this book is to provide evidence that targets are causing vast amounts of waste in the public sector. Targets are part of the problem, not part of the solution. The evidence is that good management is not about setting targets and then monitoring compliance, but about working on improving the systems to enable staff to deliver improvements for their customers. The good news is that implementing systems thinking should enable you to exceed your targets, cut costs and raise staff morale.

You are not asked to take this variant of systems thinking on trust or simply to accept the accounts of its application in this book. The way forward is for you to undertake small experiments within your own organisation to validate it for yourself. The next step is then for you to learn enough to be able to transform the performance of larger and more significant operations.

The big differentiator with this systems thinking method is that it starts with obtaining knowledge about how your organisation is actually functioning. Other methods assume that the problem to be solved is known. But people working inside organisations often have a fragmented view of their work, unaware of how the complete system functions. They are also unlikely to have accurate data on the exact level of overall service their customers are receiving. These two factors mean that without better analysis the correct problem will not be identified.

People who have worked for many years in an organisation are naturally sceptical when it is suggested to them that they do not fully understand how their own business works or should work. It is this challenge to your assumptions about 'good management' that is the hardest thing to accept. To experience for yourself how to significantly improve your organisation see the 'Overview' page.

The Vanguard Method uniquely combines two main components:

1. Systems Theory – how organisations work.

2. Intervention Theory – how to make successful change.

The starting point is to assume that your organisation is full of waste. The need is to identify this waste so it can be removed. This removal of waste is how the apparently conflicting goals of cutting costs, improving service and having happier staff are achieved.

While there are many different types and flavours of management, the dominant model in the UK's public sector is termed 'command and control'. This approach does work but it is inherently very wasteful. If you have spent your working life in a command and control environment you will probably assume there is no other way to manage. It then is logical for you to try to improve results by just being better at 'command and control'. Unfortunately applying more of the same usually makes matters worse.

The key characteristic is that 'command and control' organisations are driven from the top. A goal is set of, say, 3% cost reduction (Gershon Review, 2003) or of using IT to improve efficiency (Varney Review, 2006) and the organisation is obliged to respond to achieve the arbitrary target. The problem is that the target is set by people separate from the work and with no knowledge of how the work is carried out. Instead of engaging the workforce, a premium is placed on their compliance and how they perform against the target. This channels their ingenuity away from serving customers to achieving the target. Staff constantly look upwards for direction rather than outwards to their customers. This is the root cause of much bad service and low levels of innovation in the public sector.

About Systems Thinking

Systems thinking is a profoundly different way of seeing the world that is diametrically opposed to command and control, reductionist approaches to management.

Command and Control Thinking		Systems Thinking
Top-down	Perspective	Outside-in
Functional specialisation	Design	Demand, value and flow
Separated from work	Decision-making	Integrated with work
Budget, targets, standards, activity and productivity	Measurement	Designed against Purpose, demonstrate variation
Extrinsic	Motivation	Intrinsic
Manage budgets and the people	Management Ethic	Act on the system
Contractual	Attitude to customers	What matters...?
Contractual	Attitude to suppliers	Partnering and cooperation
Change by project/initiative	Approach to change	Adaptive, integral

This systems thinking approach is continually developing, having evolved from over 20 years' experience of interventions in the private sector and 10 years' experience of public sector service organisations.

Organisations and people who become interested in systems thinking have discovered it to be a powerful method for radically transforming the way that they work. Many have found this journey to be the most stimulating experience of their careers.

Systems thinking can often seem controversial and uncomfortable as it challenges many of the core paradigms of management. This is because once a new way of seeing things that works has been learnt, it is impossible to accept management mythologies that have never delivered.

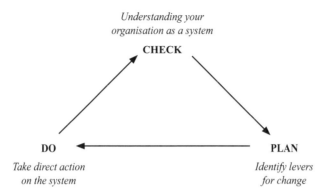

This systems thinking method is a powerful way for you to reach profound knowledge about your system, allowing you to achieve results that outstrip anything that would be set for you as a target by government.

The Vanguard System Thinking Method

This method is a form of systems thinking that acknowledges the work of precursors such as Ohno (1992), Deming (1982) and Ackoff (1987). Whilst all systems thinkers agree that a system is a sum of its parts and the parts must be rearranged as one, this approach is unique in that it starts and ends with the work. More importantly, it is a method that applies systems principles to a broad range of organisations, each yielding unimagined benefits both to people (customers and staff) and results in the form of improved performance.

Check-Plan-Do

There are three steps in performance improvement. If you know the 'what and why' of current performance, you will have confidence in planning and executing change, which is why we start at 'Check'.

The method's three-step cycle:
- understand the current organisation as a system
- identify levers for change
- take direct action on the system:

can be thought of as **Check – Plan – Do**.

Check

- Purpose: What is the purpose of this system?
- Demand: What is the nature of customer demand?
- Capability: What is it predictably achieving?
- Flow: How does the work work?
- System Conditions: Why does the system behave this way?
- Thinking: Underlying assumptions about how work is managed.

Each of the six case studies follows the above model. The place to develop your own learning is to experience 'Check' for yourself. To prepare for this, read the case studies and follow how each organisation worked through 'Check'. Apply what they found, the challenges that arose and the actions that they took, to help you experiment within your own organisation.

CHAPTER 1

EAST DEVON DISTRICT COUNCIL
HOUSING BENEFITS TRANSFORMED

Denise Lyon, East Devon District Council
Andy Brogan, Vanguard Consulting Ltd

This case study illustrates the following:

- The importance of learning about our current assumptions of how management is best carried out. The need to realise that conventional 'good management' practice may be part of the problem, not part of the solution.

- How essential it is to establish the 'purpose' of the organisation from a customer's perspective. To understand precisely what the customers need the service to provide.

- The need to understand exactly what demands are being made by customers. Particularly the level of demand that is preventable as it is caused by flaws in the existing system itself. Identifying preventable or failure demand is a first step to reducing waste while improving service.

- The realisations that the slow service and the forms provided to customers were generating many anxious phone calls. Therefore if the service was made faster and the problems experienced by customers with the forms were addressed, then performance would rapidly improve while reducing costs.

- The data showing that setting staff 'targets' was part of the problem. The problem was how the system was designed and managed. People were doing what they were employed to do. Targets are not the way to improve systems, indeed they sub-optimise a system and make performance worse.

1. EAST DEVON DISTRICT COUNCIL: HOUSING BENEFITS TRANSFORMED

Denise Lyon, East Devon District Council
Andy Brogan, Vanguard Consulting Ltd

Background

East Devon District Council is a local government organisation that employs around 520 people and serves some 64,000 households. It provides a wide range of services including: planning, licensing, refuse and recycling, environmental health, housing and housing benefits. The Council is located in the south west of England, and serves an area with beaches and natural beauty popular with holiday makers.

Housing Benefit provides financial help towards rent and some service charges for private, local authority and housing association tenants, and it is payable either to the claimant or to the landlord. There are nearly 10,000 households in East Devon claiming Housing Benefit. This results in around 2,700 new claims and changes each month which are processed by 16 employees.

Getting the benefits

Senior leaders at East Devon District Council have been learning what it means to take a systems thinking perspective to running our organisation. Working with our Housing Benefits team as a pilot area for taking a systems thinking approach we have achieved transformational results in a matter of weeks and months, not years. Even in these credit crunch times, against a back drop of constrained resource and rapidly increasing demand, our team is delivering radically improved processing times and customer satisfaction. So how are they doing it and what have we learned?

In winter 2007 we decided to adopt a systems thinking approach to all Council services, starting with our Planning and Housing Benefits services. We didn't know fully what to expect but we knew that we could not afford to maintain the status quo. Like other local authorities we were and are having to rise to the challenge of how to deliver more and better service with the same or less resource. We saw systems thinking as offering the innovative perspective and fresh thinking which we believed would be required to meet this challenge.

Great news – we were right!

What is systems thinking?

In the time we have spent learning and applying systems thinking to our organisation we have come to understand that it is an approach to how organisations design and manage their business that has far reaching implications for every aspect of organisational life. Primarily, systems thinking is a perspective from which an organisation can understand and then improve the service that it delivers to customers. However, what is so challenging and therefore what is so powerful about this perspective is that it shows much of what 'traditional' management thinking would regard as good practice to be a part of the problem not the solution.

Getting started

Our path to improvement started with getting knowledge about the 'what and why' of our current performance. Working with Vanguard Consulting we were helped to see the performance of our service from the perspective of its customers, mainly benefits claimants. We worked through a simple framework (see *Figure 1: The Vanguard Model for 'Check'*) which led us out into our service to gather data and engage with the Benefits team in understanding how their work works.

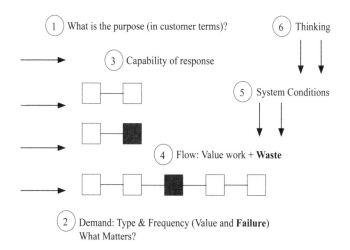

Figure 1: The Vanguard Model for 'Check'

This framework led us to ask some straightforward but profound questions about our benefits service:

- What, from a claimant's point of view, are we here to deliver – what's our purpose?

- What types of demand do our claimants make on us and what matters to them when they do so? Do we get demands as a result of us not getting things right – 'preventable demand' – and, if so, how often and for what reasons?

- How good are we at doing what we are here to do – what's our capability to meet purpose?

- Are our processes designed to do only what they must to meet purpose or is there 'waste'? If so, how much 'waste'?

- If things aren't perfect then what's holding us back and causing 'waste' and 'preventable demand' – what are the 'system conditions' impacting the work?

- If things aren't perfect then why do we choose to design and manage the service this way? How will we need to change our thinking in order to improve?

What we discovered revealed a picture of performance quite different from that which we were used to seeing in our executive board reports and in other management information. Whilst we had not been blind to the fact that there was scope for improvement it was also true that we had not fully understood the extent of the opportunity (and need) for improvement.

The 'Check' team

The team that carried out the intervention was:

Simon Davey   Head of Finance

John Cooper   Revenues and Benefits Manager

Elaine Brett   Principal Benefits Officer

Gemma Corps   Benefits Assessor

Linda Gillespie   Benefits Assessor

Jamila Lodge   Customer Service Advisor

They worked three days a week for five weeks on the 'check' part of the process. The Housing Benefit Team Leaders worked half a day a week shadowing the work of the 'Check' Team. The 'Check' Team was supported by Tony Rubbra (Vanguard Consulting) and Denise Lyon (Deputy Chief Executive).

Learning to see – the 'what' of our performance

Our eyes were first opened when we began to understand the nature of demand coming into the service.

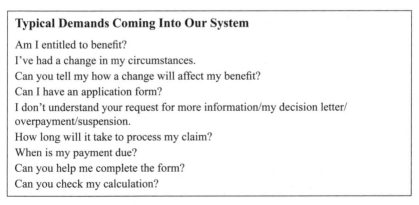

> **Typical Demands Coming Into Our System**
>
> Am I entitled to benefit?
> I've had a change in my circumstances.
> Can you tell my how a change will affect my benefit?
> Can I have an application form?
> I don't understand your request for more information/my decision letter/ overpayment/suspension.
> How long will it take to process my claim?
> When is my payment due?
> Can you help me complete the form?
> Can you check my calculation?

Figure 2: Demand Types coming into the Benefits System

We looked at demand over a number of weeks with staff from the service and together we asked, 'Why are we getting this?' The result: 42% of demand placed on the service arose because our system had either failed to do something or to do something right for our customers. If only we could learn how to deliver what mattered to our customers – how to meet their 'value' demands optimally – then we could stop this 'preventable' demand and release capacity to focus on providing more of what matters. The analysis was even more compelling when we looked at demand data by channel.

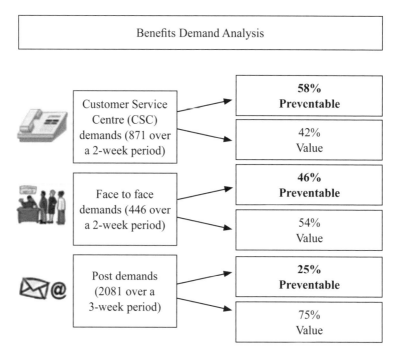

Figure 3: Benefits System Demand Analysis

The picture of performance built rapidly as we looked deeper into different aspects of our service to customers. Speaking to our customers had revealed a clear pattern of what really mattered to them. They told us that they wanted:

1. A kind, caring person to help them out
2. A quick decision
3. To be kept informed

4. To have forms and processes that are clear and easy to understand
5. To be only asked once for all the information up-front so that the process goes smoothly and claimants get what they are entitled to

We seemed to be getting point 1 right, but in each of the other four key areas (points 2-5) we were failing to perform and so were driving in preventable demands. For example, long and widely varying processing times (see *Figure 4: End-to-End Capability for New Claims*) were resulting in 36% of the preventable demand being received by our Customer Service Centre (CSC) in the form of queries from claimants asking how long their claim would take or when their payment was due.

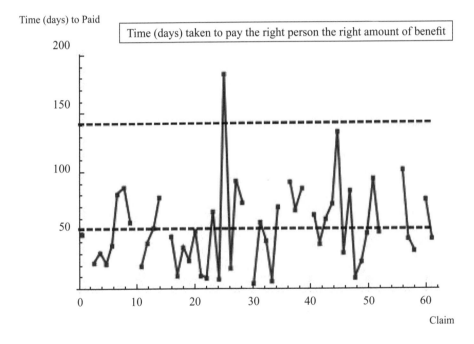

Figure 4: End-to-End Capability for New Claims

Meanwhile a further 36% of preventable demand into the CSC was from claimants telling us that they didn't understand our communication (letters, decision notices, etc). We quickly understood that being one of our customers must often be a frustrating and anxiety-inducing experience.

Learning to see – the 'why' of our performance

So we knew with alarming clarity that our service had scope for improvement but we needed to understand how to improve it. This took us into an examination of our processes of work, where we sought to understand how work was flowing and where our processes were breaking down.

As we sampled cases and explored our processes, making links to the demand data, it became obvious that we had made a simple system complex, with predictable consequences for performance. In stark contrast to the simplicity with which we were able to characterise what our service was there to do (pay the right person the right amount of benefit at the right time) we found processes of work that propagated confusion and complexity.

And yet the people in these processes of work, the Benefits team, were by-and-large doing what they had been employed to do. They were opening, sorting, logging and allocating the post. They were pre-assessing and assessing claims. They were ensuring that claimants had submitted all of the information that we required and notifying them when they had not. In short, they were doing what the current system required them to do.

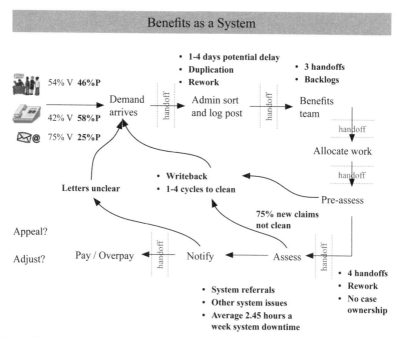

Figure 5: Benefits as a System

This was another pivotal point in our systems thinking journey. What we were starting to learn was that the received wisdom that governed the design and management of our benefits service was wrong. We did not have a 'people' issue, we had a system design and management issue. In particular:

- We had split work into functions for presumed greater efficiency. (But this had led to hand-offs, rechecking and therefore delay.)

- We had believed that it was less stressful and more efficient that no individual member of staff own a claim.
(But this had led to rework each time the same claim was picked up.)

- We had decided that some specific jobs should only be done by one individual for consistency.
(But this caused delays when they were not available.)

- We didn't allow new starters to join the team fully for 12-18 months to ensure accurate decisions.
(But this caused operational capacity issues.)

- We actively looked for fraudulent information and claims to make sure we paid the right people the correct amount.
(But this led to over-specification and rework.)

- We let unclean applications into our system in order to get the process started.
(But this led to writebacks and time delays.)

Perhaps most remarkable of all though was that each of these issues had spent so long 'under the radar'. These 'logics' which were driving our system were invisible to us until we learned how to look. They did not appear in our structure charts. They did not appear in our policies and procedures. They were not there in our performance indicators and management reports and yet they were implicit and making their presence felt in each. Our journey through 'Check' had revealed to us not just the inadequacy of our service to customers but also the inadequacy of our methods of management.

Turning the corner

We now understood how our thinking needed to change if we were to improve our performance. Taking a systems approach had revealed to us not just the scope of opportunity but also where the key levers for improvement in the system were. We set out to experiment with new ways of working focused on doing only and always the value work involved, namely:

- Getting accurate, complete and 'clean' information
- Giving good advice so that customers understood:
    - Timescales of when they will get a decision
    - The likelihood of them getting benefit
    - The progress of their claim
- Advising customers of decisions, including reasons
- Paying the right amount of benefit

Surrounding this new focus we built new measures and new principles that would help us and those working in the service to continue to identify and work on the issues that impacted our capability to pay the right people the right amount of benefit at the right time.

This involved change for senior leaders, managers and front line staff in equal measure. The way in which we were all spending our time was about to change dramatically.

Becoming a systems thinking service

East Devon DC is like most other organisations. We have our governance arrangements, our committees, our management meetings, our supervision and appraisal frameworks and so on. What we had learned in 'Check', though, was that none of these were systematically identifying or addressing the root causes of problems affecting performance in our system. Now we had to address how we managed ourselves as well as how we delivered our services. This meant changing the relationship between front line delivery and our management infrastructure. In particular, it meant being clear that it is everyone's job to understand and improve our services and that this is not a task to be delegated or managed at arm's length. 'Check' had revealed to us that our performance was being driven by the system design and not the people working in it. What use then would setting targets for improvement be unless we were prepared to change the system? Improvement, we were clear, meant everyone rolling up their sleeves and getting their hands dirty: so that is what we did.

For senior leadership and service management 'rolling our sleeves up' meant getting a handle on new and better measures of performance and using these constantly to question and understand the service. These measures had to relate to what mattered to our customers and had to demonstrate variation in our performance over time. We had learned that measuring anything else simply served to distract our attention from the real opportunities for improvement.

With better measures in place the conversations at all levels started to change, as did the relationships. Because the management infrastructure was now focused on root causes and what mattered to customers, staff found themselves better supported and therefore more willing to engage. We adopted an issues log which was available for all to fill in and which provided transparency about what factors were affecting performance and what action was being taken to address these. This put our staff and our management 'on the same team' – as they should be – collectively and individually focused on the opportunities for improvement.

Underpinning all of this was a new understanding – that the role of leadership and management is to help staff to find solutions to the problems affecting performance. Whilst this sounds obvious we had discovered that our old ways of working actually treated staff as if they were the problem or else made management treat the hierarchy as the 'customer' to be served. Our new focus put leadership and management at the service of both their team and, ultimately, the true customer: those using our services.

Amidst all of this something remarkable was happening. Our culture was changing and our management activities were becoming ever more targeted and ever more effective. The journey towards a systems thinking approach had started to drive waste and failure not just from our service delivery processes but also from our management processes. We were starting to feel like a new organisation.

It's getting better all the time

When we started out on our systems thinking journey we were providing a service that was behind the pace. Benchmarking against other local authorities saw our service positioned in the bottom quartile of the national league tables. Processing times for our two main value demands into the service were poor, despite much previous effort and some previous improvement:

- Average processing time for new claims (2007/08) = 36 days

- Average processing time for changes in circumstance (2007/08) = 20 days

In May 2008, following our work to understand our service as a system, we created a small team focused on trialling new ways of working within a framework of new principles and new measures.

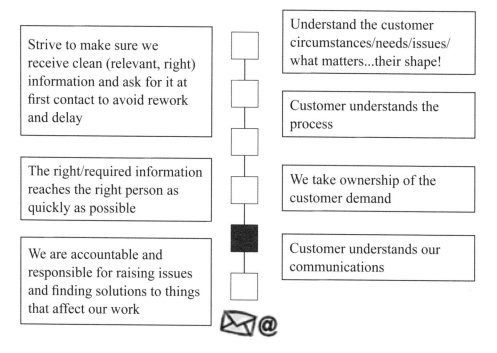

Figure 6: East Devon District Council's Systems Thinking Principles for Housing Benefits

The results were remarkable. By July 2008 our processing times within the redesign team had dropped to 6 days for new claims and 3 to 4 days for changes in circumstance. Customer satisfaction ratings for those using the new system were at unprecedented levels (9.3 out of 10). This experimentation / prototyping phase showed what was possible. The next test was to see the performance levels that could be achieved in January 2009 when the redesign was rolled-in to the whole operation.

But this was only half the story because the redesign team were now in the habit of improvement, of taking ownership of the problems that affected their work and generating solutions. The creativity unleashed was powerful and we were soon into trialling tele-claims, handling low-risk changes by phone and working with staff in other areas (such as reception) to help them to help our customers.

We were all growing in confidence and so it was time to move out of the safety of our experimentation phase into trialling these new ways of working 'in the wild'. In January 2009 we rolled in our whole service to the new design and again the results were striking:

- Average processing time for new claims before roll-in (down from 36 days before experimentation) = 26.8 days

- Average processing time for new claims after roll-in = 16.9 days

- Average processing time for changes in circumstance before roll-in (down from 20 days before experimentation) = 16.3 days

- Average processing time for changes in circumstance after roll-in = 3.8 days

- Preventable demand before roll-in = 42%

- Preventable demand after roll-in = 5%

- Average cost to process a claim (2007/08) = £102.31

- Average cost to process a claim (2008/09) = £93.00
  (NB Only part year effect of new methods on cost per claim since we only rolled-in during Q4)

Once again though, the numbers only tell half the story. The backdrop to our remarkable improvement was the financial Armageddon of the credit crunch and ensuing recession. This sent new claims demand skyward but still we improved.

Moreover, during roll-in and beyond, our team carried two vacancies. In our old system this would have spelled disaster – we just wouldn't have coped without investing more resource. However, the success of our redesign work had removed so much waste and preventable demand from our system that we continued to deliver improvement despite these new challenges.

Perhaps most striking of all then, is that our transformational service results have been delivered whilst using 6.5% less resource to handle 33% more work. That, by any measure, is improvement you can believe in.

Conclusion

Service change is never easy, still less so when it means questioning and changing the fundamental assumptions and beliefs that drive an organisation. There have been times (many of them) where those involved in developing our new organisation have needed support and encouragement. However, we believe that our results speak for themselves. What is more, we know that our improvement journey is not over. In adopting a systems thinking approach to our organisation we have started to hard-wire a new framework for leadership, management and service delivery which we know will keep us improving into the future. It is with confidence therefore that we have embarked on further systems thinking service change in other areas of our business using our new principles for leadership and management.

Leaders:
- Champion the principles of challenge and improvement.
- Are accountable and responsible for improvement.
- Use measures and knowledge to support improvement and make change happen even during difficult times.
- Help management through change and in tackling obstructions – both operational and behavioural.
- Prioritise open, consistent and frequent communication.
- Keep clear on Purpose and protect the team from other pressures.
- Work with staff to find solutions to externally driven change.
- Understand the system and the issues currently being worked on.
- Are available on 'pull' to make the work work.

Figure 7: East Devon District Council's Systems Thinking Principles for Leadership

Managers:
- Focus on our customers
  - Understand what we are being asked for or told
  - Understand what's important to them.
- Make sure there is clarity of Purpose and Principles throughout our teams.
- Use Measures that inform and guide us in improving our Capability to meet Purpose.
- Work with our teams to design the processes that deliver service in the most efficient and effective way
  - Make sure the skills, knowledge and expertise are in the right place to deal with demand
  - Make sure the tools are available
  - Understand the capacity to make sure that the relevant resources are available.
- Work with our teams to tackle issues affecting their work and causes of waste and preventable demand in our processes.
- Help our teams through change and tackle obstructions – both operational and behavioural.
- Comply with regulatory and statutory obligations but challenge and strive to limit their impact.
- Make decisions based on knowledge, understanding and data, not assumption.
- Are accountable and responsible for the capability of our teams.
- Are open and honest in our communications.
- Teach our people the end-to-end process.

Figure 8: East Devon District Council's Systems thinking Principles for Management

Summary of learning

Our systems thinking journey has taught us a number of invaluable lessons but perhaps foremost amongst these are:

It's the system not the people.

When we learned how to understand our service as a system we saw that the roots of performance lay in how the service was designed and managed. The big wins therefore lay in acting on the system, not in performance-managing our people. This realisation has an important corollary: that the role of management and leadership is to help those in the work to find solutions to the problems that affect their work. When an organisation puts this thinking into action it unlocks its hidden potential.

Measure the right things or pay the price.

It's an overused phrase that 'what gets measured gets managed' but that makes it no less true. Until we understood what mattered to our customers and what, from our customers' perspective, we were there to deliver, we could not measure and therefore manage the right things. This left us reacting to symptoms rather than root causes, investing energy and resource in 'sticking plaster' solutions. In that mode, managing the service amounted to 'staying afloat' rather than going from strength to strength. Getting clear on what the right things to measure were helped us to move on.

It's a thinking thing

So much improvement effort starts by jumping into the processes of work and redesigning these as if all that anyone needs to do to improve is to draw the perfect flow chart and then get people to follow it. However, the reality of work is that it exists in three dimensions. Processes are not just series of logical steps in a flow; they are a consequence of the thinking that underpins their design and the focus that surrounds their delivery. Until the design thinking and day-to-day focus is clear and rooted in the customer, then the service that results cannot be the best possible. It is by understanding how current thinking has resulted in the current design and the current focus that a service can identify its greatest levers for change and improvement.

About the authors

Denise Lyon: Deputy Chief Executive. Denise's role for the last 2 years has been to drive a step change in transforming customer service using systems thinking principles.

East Devon Council, Council Offices, Knowle, Sidmouth, EX10 8HL

Tel: 01395 517446   Email: DLyon@eastdevon.gov.uk
www.eastdevon.gov.uk

Andy Brogan: Over a number of years working as an employee in local authorities and the NHS I came to realise that common approaches to improvement weren't getting to the root of the problem. This often resulted in organisations only learning how to do the wrong things righter. During this time I witnessed first-hand the pressures and constraints that leaders and staff in these organisations were routinely subject to and how unhelpful these often were. In 2004 I had the good fortune to learn about systems thinking and to discover the Vanguard Method. Since then I have been employing this learning and method to help organisations to deliver truly transformational results.

Consultant, Vanguard Consulting Ltd, Villiers House, 1 Nelson Street, Buckingham, MK18 1BU

Tel: 0128 0822255   Email: andy.brogan@vanguardconsult.co.uk
www.systemsthinking.co.uk

CHAPTER 2

STROUD DISTRICT COUNCIL
SYSTEMS THINKING: RESULTS IN HOUSING BENEFITS

Anne McKenzie, Stroud District Council

This case study illustrates the following:

- A low cost, low risk start to improvement can be made by simply analysing why customers contact an organisation. This quickly provides data on how much waste there is in the system which can be a powerful catalyst for change.

- The counter-intuitive act of putting more resources at the start of a process to ensure only correct work enters the system can produce considerable savings in time and processing effort.

- Change may well falter if the people who work with the systems daily are not part of the change and continual improvement processes.

- Starting from the clear objective of fulfilling customer expectations as quickly and efficiently as possible gives a clear focus for process redesign decisions.

- Staff now have a sense of accomplishment and pride in their work, reflected in sickness levels falling by 44%.

2. STROUD DISTRICT COUNCIL
SYSTEMS THINKING: RESULTS IN HOUSING BENEFITS

Anne McKenzie, Stroud District Council

Background

Stroud District Council is a local government organisation that employs around 360 staff and serves some 49,000 households. It provides a broad range of services including: Housing, Refuse & Recycling, Regeneration, Planning and Leisure. The Council is situated in the Cotswolds in the south west of England.

Housing Benefit provides financial help towards rent and some service charges for private, local authority and housing association tenants, and it is payable either to the claimant or to the landlord. The maximum payable is 100% of the 'eligible' rent. Eligible charges include items such as: general management costs, charges for furniture and cleaning of communal areas.

How we started

In 2006, the Stroud District Council participated in bidding for and delivering aspects of the Gloucestershire Capacity Building Programme. As part of this programme, the six District Councils and Gloucestershire County Council decided to undertake joint training in systems thinking and managing change. The overall aim was to improve customer focus, drive out waste and improve process flows.

About 80 of the senior managers in the county ranging from Chief Executives and Heads of Service to Unit Managers met fortnightly for six sessions to learn about the fundamentals of systems thinking. We formed teams and after each session carried out homework in each other's authorities, practising our skills in 'Check' – analysing demand for a service and assessing how much of it was value and how much was 'waste' or work that had no real value to the customer.

Stroud trained 13 members of staff including David Hagg, our Chief Executive. When the initial training was completed, six projects were identified as suitable for us to practise our new skills in. Pairs of trainees were each allocated a project with the Chief Executive overseeing the projects.

Housing Benefits was an obvious area as it had already undergone so many changes, most of which had been simply added on to an existing process. Despite a lot of hard work, we were struggling to sustain any improved performance. We put together a team of six volunteers from Benefits, Revenues and the Head of Modernisation & ICT to begin the process. Having volunteers who knew little about the process of assessing Benefits helped enormously as they brought fresh ideas to the table.

First stages

The Housing Benefit section employs around 19 people and serves approximately 8,300 clients. It is responsible for distributing in excess of £32 million in Housing and Council Tax benefits.

The team defined the purpose of the service as 'to pay the right amount of Housing Benefit to the right person at the right time'. We then analysed all the demands customers made on the service by phone, mail, email and personal visits and the initial 'Check' showed a shocking 90% waste or failure demand.

Much of this was due to customers progress-chasing their claims, telling us that they did not understand some of the correspondence they received and, by far the most frequent, incomplete claim forms.

Customers coming to the office were seen by generic Customer Service staff who had been trained in the basics of Housing Benefits. Because of the complexity of the subject, Housing Benefit assessors were finding that customers hadn't been asked for the correct information or documents and we had to write to them for further information. This was frustrating for the customers and added considerably to the time it was taking to assess their benefits.

At Stroud, we use a Document Image Processing and workflow system (DIP), with staff being allocated work from a general electronic queue. Every incoming document was scanned to the system and would be routed electronically as either a new item of work or to join an existing claim if previous documents had been received.

Past practice was to look at a claim, send out a letter asking for any missing information, making the case pending until the information arrived and then moving on to the next case. Although the assessors were doing a great deal of work, little was completed on the first attempt.

Because of the systems in place, assessors believed themselves to be 'processors' and made little or no person contact with our claimants. A single claim could, in a significant proportion of cases, be looked at up to 7 or 8 times before being completed, with letters and responses often crossing in the post and deadlines being missed and reset.

In what seemed like a counter-intuitive move, we took an assessor away from an already busy team and put them out in our reception. By trying to get the process right at the beginning, it stopped some of the waste getting into the system.

We also realised that 40% of the claim forms we sent out weren't being returned. We contacted many of the customers to find out why. It became obvious that had we asked the right questions at the first point of contact, we would have been able to resolve many of the queries right away. A large proportion of customers asking for claim forms really just wanted to know whether or not they were likely to get benefit for a new home they were considering renting and thought that the application form would tell them. We now give these details as a matter of course.

More worrying was the small proportion of applicants who took one look at the form and decided that it was too difficult to complete. Despite making the form as simple as possible (we have the Crystal Mark for plain English) many people are daunted by the idea of filling in any form. We started to offer home visits to help with completing the form and to make sure we had all the information we need to assess the claim.

However, in hindsight, we redesigned the system in a piecemeal fashion rather than fully understanding and embracing the principles of systems thinking. The managers became too involved with the redesign so the benefits team were not fully on board and felt no ownership of the new way of working.

From January 2008 to July 2008, a backlog started to develop and the team reverted to the old familiar ways of doing things, so although performance had improved considerably it was not sustained. Incomplete claims were set aside to wait for more information and pending queues started to lengthen.

Re-launch of systems thinking in Housing Benefits

After advice from our consultant, Richard Davies, we relaunched the project in June 2008 by asking for 3 volunteer assessors to work in isolation from the main team to redesign the process completely. Their brief was to fulfil customers' expectations by paying their benefit in the quickest, most efficient way possible.

No benefit claim form was sent out unless this small team had spoken to the customer first. They spent considerable time on the telephone with each customer, using a 'quick check' method with a spreadsheet developed by the team to see if the customer was likely to be awarded benefits.

They didn't 'gate-keep' the benefits process – anyone who wanted to make a claim was welcome to do so – but since we started this new process, our unsuccessful claims have dropped from 652 in 2007/8 to 384 in 2008/9: a 41% reduction. The team felt that it was unfair to ask someone to go through the process of completing a lengthy claim form, finding and providing the relevant documents only to be told at the end of the process that they didn't qualify.

However, if they felt that the claimant might qualify they went through their income with them in detail and sent a claim form partially completed with a personalised letter telling them exactly what documents and proofs they would need to supply. They encouraged customers to come and see them straight away, guaranteeing to assess their claim the same day if they brought all the right information with them.

All of the assessors in the main team were invited to join the team for a few days, getting one-to-one training in this new way of working. Once this small team was sure that the system was robust, they rejoined the main office and rolled out the new way of working to the rest of the section.

At first there was scepticism from other assessors, mostly based on the premise that they didn't have the luxury of being able to spend so much time with each customer while there was so much outstanding work to do. Slowly everyone realised that by spending more time getting it right at the start of the process, they rarely had to revisit the same piece of work, thus freeing them to concentrate on new claims.

Customers were encouraged to come to the office to meet with the assessor they had spoken to initially, who would help them to complete the process – unheard of at that time because our assessors considered themselves to be backroom staff. Our customers started to develop a personal relationship with the assessors and many admitted that they wouldn't have completed the claim form without their help. We are now finding that if their circumstances change later on, they will come back to the same assessor with their details as they feel that they know them and are comfortable dealing with them.

Anyone who was unable to come to us was offered a home visit, either by an assessor, one of our visiting officers, or housing officers if documents needed to be delivered or collected.

Almost all of our reminding and chasing is now done by telephone rather than by letter. Thanks to our Modernisation & ICT team, we also send text messages to claimants via the benefit system. Our younger claimants find this an easier way to communicate and it invariably produces an instant response.

We didn't realise how slavishly we worked for the DIP system, rather than using it to work for us. This was highlighted by one typical case, when notification of a minor change of circumstances was handed in to our offices. It would have taken less than a minute to process there and then, but instead it went through the indexing, scanning process and ended up on an assessor's queue about 5 days later. All complete claims and changes of circumstance that come in through our front desk are now processed from the paper claim form and the paperwork is sent to scanning as completed, with no further work necessary.

Every time we hit a block, we called in the help we needed to resolve it. We worked with our audit team, explaining what we were doing and why, so that they would have confidence in the new system.

We still have a benefit assessor in reception who deals with general benefit enquiries, but the rest of the team take it in turns to deal with customers face to face, so we no longer have a 'front office, back office' split.

The Benefits team feel complete ownership of this new system because they designed it themselves. When they come across new problems, they work out innovative ways of resolving them and only ask the managers to get involved when they hit 'blocks'. The blocks were a mixture of legislative (thinking we had to do something when really it was just custom and practice), system problems (the systems needed to work in a different way) or even officers within the team or in other sections not understanding what we were trying to do.

Everything is designed around the customer and no wasted process is allowed into the system. If it doesn't add value, we don't do it. We don't set targets for the individual assessors – each claim takes as long as it takes. The only thing we ask is that they 'get one – do one', making sure that every possible avenue is followed to complete the assessment at the first point of contact. Accuracy is also at an all time high. The last four quarterly checks all showed 100% accuracy.

Capacity

Like all Housing Benefits sections during this difficult economic downturn, we are a growth industry. There has been a huge increase in workload (about 12% in the last year), which continues to grow on a weekly basis. However, despite this, we are assessing new claims in a much shorter time and have not yet had to take on additional staff to cope with the extra workload. With the efficiencies found by removing most of the waste from the system, we can use our precious resources in creative and innovative ways.

Our visiting officers are taking turns on the front desk, freeing up the assessors to spend more time with their customers. They know they are making a positive contribution and are developing and extending their skills.

Working with Job Centre Plus, we have been holding on-site benefit clinics for companies who have to reduce their working hours or even make redundancies. By being proactive, we are able to get help to the people who need it right at the start and visiting them at work causes the least possible disruption to production. We start with a visit to the management and HR sections within companies, getting detailed information about the number of staff affected and a timetable of events, then tailor a package around them.

We are working closely with the homeless prevention team, fast tracking claims and offering discretionary housing payments where necessary.

Our Benefits team work with the Housing team and are now part of the sign-up process for new tenants. If the tenant is an existing claimant, Housing will complete a single page change of address form. If the tenant is a first time claimant, someone from the Benefits team will meet them when they come to sign up for their property and fill out a claim form with them. We are also undertaking targeted benefit take-up campaigns based on intelligence received from the Housing Officers.

Before we started systems thinking, we often took between 40 and 45 days to process a claim; now most claims are completed within a week, even with the additional workload, and 20% of them are completed within 2 days.

Customer feedback

Customers love the new way of working and the team often receive letters of thanks and even flowers. Complaints are rare and are usually about the benefits legislation rather than the way their claim has been handled. Phone calls from customers chasing the progress of claims have all but disappeared as people know that an assessor is personally handling their claim, which gives them confidence in the process.

One customer wrote:

> *'I've always had a fear of any kind of authority and found it a bit daunting to go down to the Council offices. To my surprise, I found you approachable, helpful and considerate. I feel I owe you thanks for the way you helped me...'*

Another customer, having made an unsuccessful claim three years ago, contacted us again to make another claim due to her change in circumstances. She was shocked and delighted to learn that her new claim would be assessed in two or three days, rather than the two months that it took us the last time.

Customers who do not qualify for Housing or Council Tax benefits have appreciated the straightforward advice and, where appropriate, have been signposted to other agencies that may be able to help them.

Staff feedback

There have been other unexpected bonuses too. Sickness within the team has reduced by 44%. Despite their initial reluctance, members of staff are enjoying the personal contact with their customers and feel a sense of accomplishment when resolving benefit claims quickly and efficiently.

They see their role differently too. They have changed from 'assessing benefits' to 'helping people to claim benefits', a profound and satisfying difference.

- Quotes from the team:

    - *'Someone rang me just to thank me this morning. They didn't want anything. They just wanted to thank me. I've worked here for 8 years and that's never happened before. I was so surprised I didn't know what to say'.*

    - *'Now I remember why I come to work in the morning'.*

    - *'There's a sense of freedom in being able to work this way – we get to decide how we can resolve any problems. We don't have to ask permission to try something different'.*

The team have become intensely proud of the work they are doing and are recognised by councillors and senior management for their 'can do' attitude. We have just hosted a visit from the managers of a Welsh authority who were about to embark on the same journey as us. They had concerns that their staff were anxious about the process so we arranged for their assessors to come and shadow ours for a day. They left full of enthusiasm and ideas and hopefully they too will enjoy the challenge of reshaping the way they work.

About the author

 Anne is the Head of Revenue & Benefits at Stroud District Council. Her teams deal with Housing and Council Tax Benefits, the billing and collection of Council Tax, Business Rates and Benefit overpayments, Benefit Fraud investigation, homelessness, homelessness prevention, housing advice and housing allocations. She joined SDC in 1976 having previously worked for, amongst others, Lancaster City Council, Lufthansa and ICI.

Stroud District Council, Ebley Mill, Stroud, Gloucestershire, GL5 4UB
Tel: 01453 754006   Email: anne.mckenzie@stroud.gov.uk

CHAPTER 3

STOCKPORT METROPOLITAN BOROUGH COUNCIL IMPLEMENTING SYSTEMS THINKING IN IT AND HR

Jo Lane, Stockport Metropolitan Borough Council
Phil Badley, Stockport Metropolitan Borough Council

This case study illustrates the following:

- The continual pressure from central government to improve services and cut costs.

- The need for leadership rather than just administration. The need for tactical skill to build genuine support for a change initiative. Integrating systems thinking within the leadership training programme.

- That 'systems thinking' is not a project; it is a permanent change in management thinking. It is the realisation that to achieve better results will require changes in thinking and acting. To sustain this will have implications for recruitment, promotion and training.

- The personal risks and challenges of adopting a different way of doing things. Specifically the motivation for busy senior managers whose operations have been audited and found 'excellent' to involve themselves in finding out how the work is actually carried out.

- The emergent nature of systems thinking. The starting point is not a plan, but rather spending time with front line work to obtain specific knowledge of the reasons for the demands on the system. It is a radically different starting point.

- The difficulty of organisations being rewarded for following advice from central government when the advice was found to be inappropriate and harmful.

3. STOCKPORT METROPOLITAN BOROUGH COUNCIL: IMPLEMENTING SYSTEMS THINKING IN IT AND HR

Jo Lane, Stockport Metropolitan Borough Council
Phil Badley, Stockport Metropolitan Borough Council

Background

Stockport Council, a metropolitan authority in the north west of England, has a population of approximately 290,000. With a net annual revenue budget of £330m and a full and part-time staff of around 10,000 people (including those based in schools), the Council is a major organisation and the biggest employer in the borough.

Stockport Council had demonstrated sustained improvements in performance over a number of years, achieving 'excellent' status in 2005 and adding 'improving strongly': the highest rating under the national Audit Commission inspection framework in 2008. However, despite these 'accolades', given the developing national context, the Council still faces huge challenges lying ahead. These arise from immense governmental pressures on the public sector to improve and become more efficient. Hence, 'transformation' is now a common theme across local government.

Context

The Local Government and Public Involvement in Health Act (2007), the Comprehensive Spending Review 2007 (CSR07) and major public service reviews, carried out by Sir David Varney (2006), Sir Peter Gershon (2004), and Sir Michael Lyons (2004) have all highlighted the need to improve the citizen's experience of public services and for local government to become more efficient.

Following the Gershon report, central government pledged to deliver £20bn worth of efficiencies over the period 2004 to 2007. Local government contributed £4.3bn of these efficiency savings and the Local Government Association reported that this had been achieved through a variety of different methods including better procurement, business process redesign, shared services, improved use of assets and more effective use of technology.

The Government then set an ambitious target of 3% annual efficiency savings in the 2007 Comprehensive Spending Review period, 2008–2011 (CSR07). A Service Transformation Agreement (STA) was also launched as part of the CSR07 to change 'public services so they more often meet the needs of people and businesses, rather than the needs of government and by doing so reduce the frustration and stress of accessing them'.

The Audit Commission's report 'Front to Back: Efficiency of Back Office Functions in Local Government' (2008), warned local authorities not to be complacent. This report stated that 'Local government is expected to achieve £4.9bn cash releasing efficiencies by 2010/2011. Failure to make efficiency savings will mean service cuts or an inability to respond to new challenges'.

The report highlighted that 'the most successful approaches to improving back office efficiency during SR04 were redesigned business processes and improved use of Information and Communications Technology (ICT). Councils used a portfolio of internal (good housekeeping), mutual (shared services) and external (outsourced) methods for achieving back office efficiency gains'. All councils were urged to adopt these measures.

The 2008 Front Office Shared Services (FOSS) report, 'Delivering Public Service Transformation', asserted that local authorities should focus on a number of specific strategic areas to deliver the STA vision of service transformation. These included rationalising services for efficiency and service improvement, and grouping services in ways that are meaningful for the customer. Meanwhile, the Local Government and Public Involvement in Health Act (2007) provided a strong focus on empowering citizens and promoting cooperation between public service partners.

In 2007 the Government also introduced a new performance management framework for local government. This was aimed at 'replacing the range of current issue-specific performance indicator sets and reducing the reporting burden for local authorities' (CSR07). The framework has several components including a revised and reduced set of 198 indicators, including NI14, which focuses on reducing avoidable contact.

The FOSS report states that 'Effective action on NI14 will require a good understanding of customers' needs, the reasons why they contact their local authorities and the ways in which different access channels are, and could be, used. Councils will need to review their internal processes to understand the value that each step does – or does not – add to delivering information or services'.

To support local authorities in responding to the not inconsiderable challenges posed by all the above, a National Improvement and Efficiency Strategy (2008) has also been developed. At its core are the Regional Improvement and Efficiency Partnerships, who have been allocated £185m and tasked with helping local authorities to provide better and more efficient services. However, in terms of progress being made, the Treasury, in a recent report entitled 'Operational Efficiency Programme: Back Office Operations and IT' (2009), warns that the pace of change needs to be accelerated. This report estimates that 'the annual cost of back office operations could be reduced by around £3.2bn'. It also proposes the introduction of operational reviews to 'examine spending effectiveness and to ensure that poorer performing organisations improve … and deliver increased value for money and effectiveness'.

Given this overwhelming plethora of dictates, expectations, guidance, reviews and penalties, to say that the pressure is on public service to 'transform' is something of an understatement!

In light of the national context outlined above it is perhaps not surprising that Stockport Council's Medium Term Financial Strategy predicted a difficult financial picture – one no doubt shared by most local authorities. The Government's target for all Local Authorities to identify 3% cash releasing efficiencies per annum from 2008 to 2011, means Stockport Council must make substantial savings – estimated at more than £5million during 2008/9, £6.2million in 2009/10 and a further £3.8million in 2010/11. And this before the impact of the credit crunch in 2009! The urgency of this need has led to the development of the Council's Business Improvement, Transformation and Efficiency (BITE) Strategy (2008) which carries the full support and commitment of the organisation's Corporate Leadership Team and, importantly, the Executive – the group of councillors charged with the political leadership of the Council. The BITE strategy has a twin track approach: Efficiency (reducing spending) and Transformation (improving service delivery).

The efficiency track is focused on generating cost savings in the short and medium term. A key element is the Corporate Efficiency Plan 2009-12. This plan outlines cross-cutting and service specific priority areas for cost reduction including the way the organisation undertakes commissioning and procurement. There is also an 'invest to save' scheme which invites services to bid for monies to pursue local projects, each bid being judged on the strength of a business case that can demonstrate both service improvement and efficiency savings.

Getting started

The transformation element of the strategy, of which more below, is taking a systems thinking approach to service delivery with the aim of achieving ongoing and sustainable improvements in performance. The emphasis here is on improvement, not savings. Clearly, the efficiency strand of the BITE Strategy represents a more traditional approach to achieving savings. In contrast, the transformation element presents a more exciting, innovative, and longer term cultural and organisational development challenge.

The introduction of systems thinking to Stockport Council has had a long gestation period, taking almost two years to materialise. It followed a chance attendance in 2006 by one of the Council's senior managers at a seminar led by John Seddon. The senior manager in question, who has a wide ranging remit including organisational development, immediately grasped the potential benefit of systems thinking. However, the opportunity to showcase its capability to change the way leaders think and act within the organisation in order to drive business improvement needed to await the right opportunity.

The BITE Strategy provided that opportunity. With funding secured and having gained the initial agreement of both elected members and senior managers to pilot the systems thinking approach, the first step for the Organisation Development (OD) team was to procure the services of Vanguard Consulting. They were chosen for their clear approach and absolute commitment to transferring capability to the organisation. Secondly, the OD team established two interventions in services under their own control, Human Resources (HR), starting with the Contracts Team, and Information & Communication Technology (ICT).

This involved a steep learning curve for the OD team managers. They had to learn the Vanguard Method, lead and manage teams undertaking systems thinking interventions, showcase the approach, and continue, at the same time, to provide more traditional OD support to the rest of the organisation which, of course, continued to operate under conventional thinking. However, this proved to be the right approach, as it provided a unique perspective on the Vanguard Method from their roles as leaders in a system under review, interventionists in the making, and as tacticians seeking ways to get further buy-in to the approach from other parts of the organisation.

One of the primary differences in this systems thinking approach, compared to other transformational methodologies, is the absolute requirement for senior leaders to be not only committed, but also to take ownership of interventions within their areas of responsibility and to remain close to what is going on. The pilot interventions demonstrated that it is not possible to simply rubber stamp the strategy and then turn attention to other issues. To be successful, systems thinking needs the active intervention and support of senior leaders who are prepared to get close enough to the work itself to understand the need for change and to provide 'whatever it takes' to enable the team on the ground to improve the system. The business of getting out into the work and back to grass roots in order to support their teams through change proved to be immensely satisfying for the leaders in the ICT and HR interventions.

Building curiosity amongst middle managers has been an integral part of the approach from the start. It was recognised early on that middle managers could also help to create a groundswell of interest where the more direct approaches of the OD team to senior managers on their own might have missed the mark, given the many other claims on the attention of senior leaders. To this end, over a hundred managers have so far been through a three day Systems Thinking Fundamentals programme.

This has led to significant interest in undertaking local systems thinking improvement activity, with quite a few middle managers proving to be highly persuasive in getting their senior leaders on board. Moreover, such has been the demand for this programme that it was decided to train members of the in-house team to deliver the programme in order to provide an ongoing capability to deliver the programme in the future.

Following the success of the Fundamentals programme and the increasing levels of interest in systems thinking amongst middle managers, a corporate network has been established to help support those who are interested in learning more about systems thinking or who want to use the approach to improve their own systems, to share experiences and learning, and to generally keep the flames of interest alight.

An early imperative was to link systems thinking to internal leadership development. As the organisation took the first steps on its systems thinking journey it became increasingly clear that any such development programme must be rooted in systems thinking, given that this had been adopted as the organisation's approach to transformation. Consequently, systems thinking forms a major part of the design of a new leadership programme which is soon to be rolled out to all the organisation's 19 most senior leaders. A major outcome of the programme will be that senior leaders understand and are able to adopt the leadership role needed to embed a culture of continuous improvement using a systems thinking approach across all parts of the authority and where necessary with partners.

The Council already had a coaching strategy in place which will provide further support to the senior leaders in leading the transformation of the Council. The coaching ethos – raising awareness (of self) and taking responsibility – reflects well the requirements of leaders in systems thinking – to first understand and then act on the system.

Sustainability

A key aspect of systems thinking is sustainability, which is built in to the approach. Systems thinking is not a 'one off, tick, done it' remedy; an intervention is not a project with a life – it is for life! However, this is easy to say but what does it mean in practice? It will certainly require leaders to play their part and the notion of second and third iterations of an intervention may well escape the attention of many managers in the enthusiasm to get started once they have 'signed up' to the concept. Moreover, initial enthusiasm can easily wane over time in the face of other priorities. Therefore, the organisation is adopting a number of strategies to make sure long term sustainability ensues.

The development of internal capacity has already been mentioned. True to their commitment, Vanguard have worked continuously with the OD team to help develop the latter's capability in facilitating interventions and in running the Fundamentals programme. Soon it will be the turn of the internal interventionists to teach the Vanguard Method across the organisation and work to keep managers honest to systems thinking principles.

It is also appreciated that care needs to be taken in selecting the right leaders of an intervention 'Check' team as they have a major role further down the line in ensuring the drive for improvement does not stall. Other individuals within 'Check' teams, sometimes previously unnoticed, are also showing their true colours in terms of their aptitude for, and positive attitude towards, systems thinking. It would be a mistake if they, too, were not engaged in looking after the legacy of improvement they have played such a strong role in building.

It has been recognised that systems thinking is not just about interventions. In terms of the manager's role especially, the design and management of work in a systems thinking environment is all-pervading. For example, as the managers and employees experienced in working within interventions and a systems thinking environment leave, thought will need to be given to the kinds of people who will be recruited to take their place. Existing person specifications are unlikely to provide what the organisation will need in the future.

In terms of OD, leadership development has already been mentioned. Beyond that, in a systems thinking world, it is already evident that there are implications for Investors in People, management development, performance appraisal, competency frameworks, and 360° feedback. These are longer term issues to be addressed when the transformation of the organisation is well under way. However, it is clear that systems thinking will significantly impact how leaders and managers of the future are recruited and developed – traditional approaches will no longer be 'fit for purpose'.

Stockport began its systems thinking journey by undertaking two interventions in the ICT and HR support services which are part of the Council's Business Services Directorate. Whilst these interventions are at different stages of completion, they have both already demonstrated that a systems thinking approach does lead to significant service improvements, not to mention, as will be seen, improved employee morale, improved customer satisfaction and significant financial savings.

In the 'Check' phase the ICT intervention uncovered some startling findings about the experience of customers calling the Service Desk to report IT faults and problems. For example, the frontline service desk only resolved 17% of the calls at the point of contact, the other 83% being passed on to specialist teams. Service Desk tasks were passed to another member of staff on average 3.6 times before being resolved. The average end-to-end completion time for any job was 11.2 days. But, of course, established targets were being met!

Compare these figures to the outcomes from the Redesign phase. The frontline service desk now resolves 80% of the calls first time with only 20% being passed to other staff. The average number of pass-ons was reduced 66% from 3.6 to 1.2. The average end-to-end time of one stop jobs is now 1 day, and for jobs passed on it is 3 days. A vast improvement!

As well as greatly improving service delivery, the ICT intervention has already delivered financial savings of £120,000 with more expected as the intervention completes its first round of 'make normal'. These initial savings have been achieved through natural turnover of employees for whom it was no longer necessary to recruit replacements. This was only possible due to the removal of waste from the system which thus increased the capacity of the remaining employees. The whole team are now multi-skilled and able to deal, one-stop, with a wide variety of predictable demands.

Significant improvements have also been demonstrated within HR. The objective for the intervention was to ensure that the current workflows were designed to meet customers' future requirements in advance of the procurement of replacement HR/Payroll software. This action is unusual in itself because most IT procurement exercises usually end up with internal processes having to fit the way the technology works, rather than meeting the needs of the internal workflow. The exercise has been made more challenging because three councils are working together to procure a common system.

The HR intervention within Stockport initially focused on the Contracts and Payroll Teams which deal with changes to allowances, hours of work, honoraria, changes to posts, pay, etc. These represent the largest volume of demand placed on the HR system. Outcomes include an increase in one-stop processing of changes, which is now running at 86%, with 77% being completed on the day of receipt and 97% paid right first time for changes impacting on pay. End-to-end time for completion of changes is currently 16 days compared to 35 days before redesign, a more than 50% reduction.

The Contracts and Payroll 'Check' team has seen an impressive upturn in positive feedback from customers regarding the speed and level of service received since redesigning their workflow. This has been most noticeable in a dramatic change for the better in their relationship with schools. They are delighted that they are regularly given positive comments from the schools on the excellent service they now receive.

Both the IT and HR interventions have led to improvements in employee morale. This is most evident within HR, where a recent survey demonstrated that employees feel more valued, and part of a team where their opinions and contributions count; they are now more likely to suggest ideas that would make a difference or could lead to further improvements to service delivery. Many members of the team said that, since the newly designed processes have been implemented, they regularly receive praise and recognition for good work from their customers. Similar results were found from a similar employee survey undertaken within ICT although here the new ways of working have given rise to a certain amount of angst for some. It is expected that, with careful leadership, this will disappear once people have fully made the transition and stop grieving for the past.

There is no denying that systems thinking has proved to be quite challenging to deploy – no one said it would be easy! However, these two interventions have amply demonstrated the potential systems thinking has to revolutionise both the way the authority thinks about the design and management of work and the level of service experienced by Stockport's citizens. Moreover, whilst the application of systems thinking has, thus far, been restricted to support services, this situation will soon change.

'Scoping' – defining the area to be investigated – has been completed within Taxi Licensing and an intervention focusing on multi-agency working in Adult Social Care is set to start in the near future. 'Scoping' of Social Transport will take place in September and of Street Lighting in October. There is an intention to use this systems thinking approach to challenge the value added by the Council's Contact Centre strategy. Further interest has been expressed from people working in areas as diverse the welfare of children, debt collection and organising street markets. These interventions will not only take systems thinking into each major part of the organisation, but will also start to involve arm's-length organisations and partners.

Risk, challenges and tensions

It has already been mentioned that the introduction of systems thinking has not been easy. Indeed, its introduction has given rise to a number of tensions which are explored below.

The systems thinking philosophy may seem quite foreign to leaders who have developed thinking and skills within a command and control organisation. The approach is a significant departure from the traditional top down hierarchy, where management decisions are based on the upward flow of information, which does not always reflect the reality of what is happening on the ground. In many instances this traditional approach has resulted in the leader becoming disconnected and separated from the frontline day-to-day work.

As Stockport is a four star, 'improving strongly' authority and is already deemed to be successful, there is little incentive for the leaders to challenge current performance by spending time within the work in order to understand its true performance. As in many organisations, stepping outside the office and into the work is not the norm and, more than that, is a big 'ask' in the face of other competing demands. If the leaders perceive their areas of responsibility to be successful then what motivation exists for them to adopt an approach that will unsettle the current system and service?

Moreover, what would be the implications of adopting a systems approach and uncovering that an 'excellent' performing service is not as good as perceived, and how might the true performance reflect on the leader? It is highly likely that these questions will have occurred to at least some, if not all, the leadership team and few would relish having to confront an unpalatable truth in the current climate of efficiency drives. This may seem quite a risky improvement strategy to some in more ways than one and not least because of its emergent nature.

The emergent nature of systems thinking means that details about potential savings, future roles, structure, measures and ways of working only become clear over time. Many leaders are used to more conventional approaches to enabling change, which may include project plans and a detailed description of what will be delivered. In contrast, with systems thinking, whilst it will result in the removal of wasteful activities, create capacity, deliver improved service, and reduce cost, the extent of these cannot be predicted at the outset.

This has proved to be an anxious starting point for some managers and has given rise to significant levels of uncertainty about the approach for leaders on whom there is a great pressure to make efficiencies. With growing pressures to deliver improved services with fewer resources, it can be difficult and unnerving for a leader to commit both personal and operational resources to an intervention that has, at the outset, no quantifiable outcomes around improvements or savings; for many the approach would seem to be tantamount to a 'leap of faith'.

Paradoxically, far from undermining their positions, systems thinking potentially offers a way of achieving not only a transformed service, but also ongoing and sustainable improvement. It achieves this whilst at the same time releasing capacity and so providing the much needed efficiencies. Therefore, one of the biggest challenges in implementing systems thinking is how to engage leaders and secure their wholehearted commitment to the approach.

The interventions that have been carried out so far at Stockport have to some extent helped to alleviate these concerns. They have delivered improvements to customers by reducing end-to-end service times by over 50%. Significant savings were also achieved, in spite of the absence of project plans and clear outcomes at the start. It is hoped that the success of these interventions will encourage other leaders to try systems thinking in their areas. However, there is still pressure to gather further evidence to generate yet more confidence in the approach. It is expected that this will be achieved through learning from several planned interventions, identifying base-line operating and flow costs at the start and end of the process, and the integration of a strong systems thinking element into future senior leadership development programmes.

As has been previously mentioned, Stockport has also run a series of Systems Thinking Fundamentals courses for middle managers across the Council, in order to help generate curiosity and build understanding about the approach. This has sparked considerable interest amongst this group, who now appreciate the benefits systems thinking could bring to their services. Their enthusiasm has, in a number of instances, also been successful in generating the impetus for senior managers to engage with systems thinking through a number of 'scoping' exercises, with a strong potential to lead to further interventions.

There are tensions for employees too – largely combated by the skills of the leader in communicating, listening, coaching and generally supporting people through change. Employees often fear change and the unknown and can seem reluctant to adopt new ways of working. This was evidenced during the ICT intervention when, as the new processes were introduced, some members of the team were uncomfortable at the start with the growth and change in their roles and the skills now required to perform their new jobs.

Feelings of stress and dejection also surfaced during both the support service interventions when employees realised how their current thinking had led to poor performance in their system from a customer perspective. However, systems thinking is based on the belief that variation in performance is mainly due to the system and not the workers. Once people appreciated this they were able to stop being defensive and became more comfortable with phrases such as 'waste' and 'failure'.

A further challenge lay in managing some of the tensions that existed between those involved in the intervention and those left undertaking the daily operational activities. Those in the 'Check' team can easily be seen as being favoured. Therefore, it is vital to recognise openly the valuable role that employees in the current system play in maintaining existing operational functions. In the HR intervention the almost 'evangelical' enthusiasm of the 'Check' team generated by the rewarding work of redesigning their processes actually resulted in alienating some of those still working in the original system. Not surprisingly, this had a negative effect in terms of motivation and managers had to work hard to boost morale.

Tensions have also surfaced around jargon, structure and short term impact on service delivery. On the issue of jargon, systems thinking has its own language which can be extremely valuable, once the context and true meaning are fully understood and applied correctly. However, for the novice, terms such as 'failure demand' and 'waste' have sometimes proved to be confusing and emotive and there is a concern that they can increase initial feelings of worthlessness, blame and guilt. Experience has shown that it is important to ensure that everyday expressions are used at the same time as the correct terminology.

It also needs to be recognised that an intervention may have a short-term negative impact on performance. This was particularly found to be the case during the ICT intervention where performance levels temporarily dipped – leading to tensions with customers. The learning point here was that it is very important to manage expectations and so alleviate unnecessary pressure on both the intervention team and those still carrying out the work in the old system.

Finally, the need to work with partners and arm's-length organisations in delivering services can present further challenges in adopting systems thinking. All of the work involved is not directly in the control of the lead organisation. This means that, to set up a systems thinking intervention covering all aspects of service delivery, all the parties must engage with the approach. Moreover, the relevant leaders must be prepared to understand their collective end-to-end performance from a customer perspective, and not just look at the performance of the part of the system they manage. Stockport is only just beginning to grapple with the complexities of initiating and leading systems thinking interventions in multi-organisational contexts. Two forthcoming planned interventions involving our partners will provide much needed experience and understanding about the practicalities of applying systems thinking in these kinds of environments.

Conclusion

Despite these tensions, the early signs are that systems thinking really does have the potential to deliver on what it promises – i.e. improved services and reduced costs – as has been proven in the two pilot interventions. Moreover, curiosity has been generated and take-up, though slow, is gathering pace.

There is much talk, direction and endless guidance offered from all corners of the public sector on engaging customers and improving services. There is also lots of evidence to be provided in support of third party inspections. In reality, much of this guidance appears to inhibit the notion of true improvement through the eyes of the customer. There is growing evidence to show that 'one size does not fit all'. Yet the nature of the game is for local authorities to follow the trend or direction because reward comes through assessment. There is also an expectation that authorities will have followed the guidance or best practice offered nationally in order to be rewarded appropriately.

So far, the local learning would suggest that designing the service around the needs of the customer, based upon demand, provides a much better solution. The compromise is that considerable effort is still needed to ensure that the required evidence is available to score the marks in external assessment. However, on balance, it is felt that this is a more than worthwhile price to be paid for the benefits systems thinking can bring.

About the authors

Jo Lane: Jo is currently Head of Transformation with Stockport MBC. She has worked in Local Government for many years in the fields of performance management, human resources, learning and development and transformation. In the last 18 months, Jo has been very involved with introducing systems thinking into the organisation.   Email: jo.lane@stockport.gov.uk

Phil Badley: Phil has worked within the HR profession in the Public Sector for a number of District, Borough, Unitary and Metropolitan authorities around the country in a variety of roles.

He joined Stockport Council in January 2001 as Assistant Chief Executive (HR) with a clear remit to transform the delivery of HR across the Council, and to develop organisational capacity for change. In September 2006, Phil moved to become part of a new Business Services Directorate formed to drive transformation throughout the Council. In July 2007 he became Service Director – Organisation Development, assuming strategic responsibility for the Council's IT and Human Resources functions, together with lead responsibility for business transformation. In November 2009 his remit was extended to include Customer Strategy, Customer Contact and the Registrars service for the Council.

Phil is a Chartered Fellow of the CIPD, a Member of the Chartered Management Institute, and holds post graduate qualifications in executive and business coaching.   Email: phil.badley@stockport.gov.uk

Stockport Metropolitan Borough Council, Town Hall, Edward Street, Stockport, SK1 3XE

Tel: 0161 480 4949

www.stockport.gov.uk

CHAPTER 4

SYSTEMS THINKING IN PLANNING AND ROADS

John Cooney, Central Otago District Council, Alexandra, New Zealand

This case study is included because it illustrates the following:

- The need to agree the purpose of the organisation.

- Understanding the measures used to drive and control a system is vital.

- Setting deadlines does not create good service. The need is to understand how the work flows and then improve this.

- Work upstream with customers to help them provide clean, accurate inputs for your systems.

- Understand exactly how your current system functions from a customer's perspective before planning changes.

- To achieve significantly better results does require systems thinking, rather than just tinkering with existing processes or setting targets.

4. Systems Thinking in Planning and Roads

John Cooney, Central Otago District Council, Alexandra, New Zealand

Background

Central Otago District Council (CODC) is the fourth largest local authority in New Zealand in terms of geographic area, covering 10,000 km². But it is a small local authority even by New Zealand standards in terms of the 17,000 people it serves.

Over the last three years it has been the fastest growing economy for any local authority area in NZ[1] driven by viticulture, construction and tourism development on the traditional base of farming and horticulture.

CODC responsibilities include provision of roads, water and waste services, land use and building control, recreation facilities and services, along with tourism and community development. A staff of 140 operates along with contractors to provide the services. The overall budget varies between NZ$25 million and 30 million p.a. With the exception of roads expenditure, where half is funded by a government agency and road user charges, all revenue is raised locally from rates and user fees.

Getting started

A chance referral to a website in 2005 led to transformational action within CODC based in Alexandra, which has put the organisation at the forefront of local government performance improvement in this country. However, the journey started some years before.

In 1990, a seminar by Peter R. Scholtes introduced the work of W. Edwards Deming and his claim that levels of at least 40 – 60% waste exist in organisations. Crucially this waste is a result of the system rather than of the people in the work. This observation fitted with the management experience already gained, which suggested that people generally tried to do a good job but the system obstructed them.

---

1   BERL report 2008

43

What followed was a 15-year search for a method that could, as Deming promised, eliminate this waste and provide clarity of purpose to workers. They would then be able to respond to individual customer needs right first time every time, within a framework of continuous improvement.

Various attempts were made to introduce first Total Quality Management, business process reengineering, and then a diagnostic scheme which reviewed the organisation against various criteria to determine actions necessary to improve current performance. In each case improvement did occur. However, these improvements became increasingly difficult to maintain and the results were not of the scale Deming had claimed were possible.

In 2005 John Seddon's framework for the analysis and redesign of work was discovered and it showed promise. Initially attempting to apply this with only remote assistance from Vanguard Consulting in the UK resulted in substantial early gains followed by a period of regression. Subsequent to this a commitment to learn and apply the Vanguard Method has delivered to CODC dramatic gains in performance and immediate cost reductions. Furthermore, it is clear that significant waste still exists and can be eliminated over time.

The reason for the desire to make changes to CODC was the level of growth being experienced by the district at the time. The Central Otago District had the best performing economy in New Zealand in 2008. Upward pressure on both budgets and rates as a result of this growth had led to an interest in improving productivity. Management attention had initially been focused on interrogating proposed budgets and reviewing services with the aim of reducing less valued activity. On both counts efforts to minimise increases had generally been unsuccessful. Rates had grown by an average of 10.6% in the last 5 years.[2]

This failure to make progress provided an incentive to examine other ways to improve operations. CODC has so far successfully applied the Vanguard Method to three areas: Planning and Building Consents, Roads Management and Water Services.

---

2   CODC Annual Report summaries 2004-9

Planning and Building Consents

To provide a context for this change, consent work in 2000/01 was low. The area experienced little growth with only $16 million in building consents being issued in that year, with 22 new dwellings. Planning consents numbered around 170. Within four years building consents reached around $100 million p.a. including 250 new dwellings a year. Also around 450 resource consents were being processed annually. As the volume of work had increased by at least a factor of six, the Council was buckling under the extra demand for its services.

In addition, a national problem of leaky buildings, the result of faulty designs, had caused a change in regulation, requiring extra attention and encouraging extra inspection and other risk-adverse responses from councils. Recruitment of suitably qualified building control officers became more difficult as each authority increased staff in response to a greater number of consent applications and as more hurdles were designed into processes with the aim of minimising risk. In response to this situation the Council divided the workforce into more specialised, functional units. As building control officers were difficult to recruit, other people were put into the process to complete the less technical work.

An oversight led to construction of a new dwelling within a heritage protection area without resource consent. In reaction to this, rather than appoint another building control officer (BCO) as demand continued to increase, the option was taken of transferring responsibility for analysing planning issues to a qualified planner.

Furthermore, BCOs withdrew from engagement in any non building control issue such as connections to main water services and road access. Whilst consideration of these issues was clearly of benefit to the customer, functional specialisation of the work continued to increase as the work load increased.

In an attempt to cover any customer requests due to the lack of information supplied by this fragmented service, separate information packs were included with building consent application forms. The information outlined the need to contact other parts of the Council to unearth additional project requirements. *Figure 1* below provides an outline of the process. Not surprisingly, this design for work led to customer dissatisfaction and complaint.

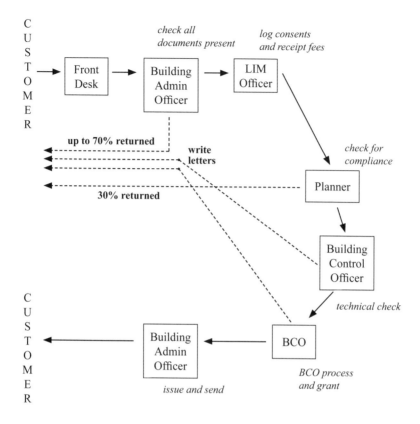

Figure 1: Building Consent Application flow before redesign

The situation was similar with resource consents. The increase in demand led to some additional recruitment and increased reliance on a consultant to complete analysis and report on applications. Internal staff members were occupied by high levels of telephone enquiries and in-person calls requesting advice about developments. Customers were also increasingly asking for progress updates and clarification concerning their applications already in the system.

It was within this situation that CODC attempted to apply the Vanguard method, beginning with the framework for 'Check' (see *Figure 2*).

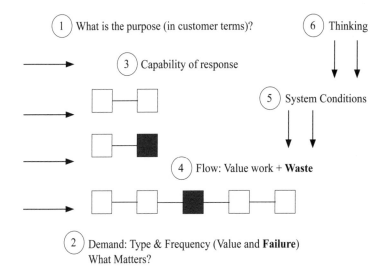

Figure 2: The Vanguard Model for 'Check'

Clarifying purpose in customer terms ignited discussion highlighting current thinking concerning the focus of the existing system. Initial suggestions for what the focus should be were: 'ensuring compliance with regulation', 'protecting Council from risk' and 'protecting the community from inappropriate action'. In the end 'to help people develop appropriately' was settled on.

Demand analysis involved listening to the contacts already being received and analysing the experience people were having as they passed through the system.

The most frequent demands from customers were:

- Where is my consent?
- What are you asking for?
- I can't understand the conditions you have applied.
- Why are fees so high?

These and other demands that were the result of the system failing to deliver what was of value to the customer – termed failure or preventable demand – made up 70% of all demand in the system.

One qualified planner discovered 85% of her work involved dealing with this failure demand. In the past, in response to such demand, CODC provided customer services training to staff. This built the capability of officers to deal with the preventable demand in a manner which placated customers rather than satisfied their needs.

An epiphany occurred as we listened to conversations with different customers. It was believed each application was a unique demand, distinct because no two consents were the same. As we listened to customers, it became apparent that different types of applicant experienced our service in obviously different ways. Experienced local surveyors had, over time, grown to understand what it took to gain consent without rework. Conversely, owners who were infrequently involved in the application process found the path to consent difficult and frustrating. Changing the focus from the application to the applicant opened opportunities for subtle variations in how the different needs were addressed.

These conversations highlighted what mattered to customers:

- Quick decision
- Smooth, easy process
- Being kept informed
- Cost effective

At that time the performance of the system was measured by counting the number of processing days it took to issue consent. This did not inform workers of their ability to deliver what mattered to customers. Processing days is a measure established by both the Building Act and Resource Management Act and only includes those working days where councils have the consent available to them to work on. Hence days when the agency is awaiting information not initially included in the application and statutory shut downs, as well as weekends, are not counted in the total.

In its place, the measure of days from initial receipt to issuing was developed. This provided a more reliable end-to-end measure of the customer experience, as it provided feedback on what mattered.

It is easy to see the connection between 'quick decisions' and 'smooth, easy processes' and improving the speed through the system. There is also a correlation between 'cost effective' and end-to-end time. This is because costs are related to work undertaken on each job and this increases the longer the work remains unfinished. It was recognised that reducing the end-to-end time would reduce the need to keep people informed concerning progress. Also, better understanding of customers' needs enabled us to keep them informed of what was needed from them at each step. Faster turnarounds were therefore anticipated.

Performance had generally averaged around the statutory targets of 20 processing days for building consents[3] and delegated resource consents. Despite this we were aware of considerable customer dissatisfaction. High levels of reworking of consent applications were discovered. Up to 70% of building consents typically required further information to be sought. Owing to the complexity of requests these averaged over a month to return. *Figure 3* provides more detailed data. Analysis of flow led to an understanding of the causes of customer dissatisfaction.

Work had been split up into the steps undertaken by a number of people dealing with different parts of the process. Building Control's front desk received the application; separate administration staff checked all documents were present and logged the consent into the IT tracking system; a planner and potentially a number of building control officers were involved in any consent.

---

3   On 1 April 2005 the statutory target for building consents rose from 10 days to 20 days. Almost immediately the Council's performance changed from an average of 10.2 days to 20.3 days as seen in *Figure 3* for the first and second six months of 2005 respectively.

Start date	End date	No. of Applications	Average Processing Days	No. with FIR [1]	FIR %	Average FIR Days	Total Working Days [2]	Customer Days [3]	% FIR of Total
01/01/05	30/06/05	471	10.16	234	50%	28.23	38.39	53.75	74%
01/07/05	31/12/05	458	20.25	270	59%	22.71	42.97	60.15	53%
01/01/06	30/06/06	455	12.51	232	51%	22.91	35.42	49.59	65%
01/07/06	31/12/06	389	12.86	274	70%	16.11	28.97	40.56	56%
01/01/07	30/06/07	503	8.74	214	43%	19.01	27.75	38.85	68%
01/07/07	31/12/07	472	12.79	220	47%	22.29	35.08	49.11	64%
01/01/08	30/06/08	465	10.62	192	41%	18.21	28.83	40.36	63%
01/07/08	31/12/08	441	5.26	134	30%	21.05	26.31	36.84	80%
01/01/09	23/06/09	383	5.58	93	24%	14.99	20.57	28.80	73%
13/05/09	23/06/09	119	5.24	18	15%	8.72	13.96	19.54	62%

Notes

1   FIR – Further information requests e.g. a request made when documentation is not complete.
2   Working days 5 days a week Monday to Friday – calculated by adding processing days to FIR days.
3   Customer days – estimate of average days elapsed in calendar days Monday to Sunday calculated by multiplying working days by 7/5.

Figure 3: Days for processing building consents 01/01/2005 – 23/06/09

When an incomplete application cycled through the system a second or subsequent time, due to a need for a Further Information Request (FIR), it was likely to be reviewed by more than one building officer. This was encouraged so that a review of the first officer's assessment was built in. Differences in interpretation led to frequent information requests which related more to an officer's personal preferences than to legal requirements. Also, feedback from customers highlighted their resignation to not getting their applications correct, which led to their just handing in poor quality applications. This in turn increased the risk of mistakes by the Council.

Given that 70% of the applications received required at least one FIR, applicants could receive a series of letters requesting different details. At each contact the official clock stopped. This allowed the Council to average 18 to 20 working days for processing consents. The real experience for customers' end-to-end time was a 54 day average, with up to 4 months being considered normal. Once this experience of multiple communications and delays was recognised it became obvious why the prevailing customer experience was unsatisfactory.

Resource consents followed a similar path. However, the ability to extend timeframes for delegated consents from 20 to 40 working days (section 37 extension) and the use of a consultant for 80% of the analysis and reporting work created longer timeframes than for building. It also ensured all internal workers were fully engaged in handling preventable demand. They were dealing with numerous customer calls concerning delayed consents and information provided to customers that they could not understand.

Of the 1015 actions which had been built into processing, from resource consent to building completion certificate, only 70 were seen as adding value to the customer. The remainder had been designed into the work to satisfy Council requirements as distinct from customer requests. These findings highlighted how the design of the system was responsible for the poor performance.

Legislation was a significant source of preventable demand. It encouraged risk aversion and the belief that statutory deadlines determined good service. Targets also drove the practice of leaving work until it became 'urgent' as time elapsed reached deadlines. Section 37 extensions were often used for resource consents and the start of processing building consents delayed until after around 16 official days had passed. This wait resulted in a surprise for the applicant when they received notice of required additional information weeks after applying. By this time the customer would have quite reasonably developed the assumption that things must be progressing and the next correspondence from Council must be the approved consent.

The dominant management belief in the Council was that efficiency improved when jobs were split into discrete tasks and allocated to different people depending on their capability. As growth occurred, this belief was acted on and the functional segmentation of the workforce was increased. Only after linking feedback from customers to flow did the adverse effects of splitting work into specialised functions become apparent.

Information made available to customers was found to be overly technical and voluminous. This was due to:

- Bad experiences encouraging the Council to write customer guidance notes to cover any significant past hurt.

- A belief that if people did not understand the consent processes it was helpful to provide them with extensive information about the Resource Management Act rather than specific information about their project.

- Providing uniform information as a means to pass the responsibility back to customers for understanding Council processes including references to other requirements outside the immediate function. The alternative would be to directly assist customers to understand all the constraints relevant to their project.

The link between the Council providing the wrong type of information and 70% of applications requiring further information requests was made. Previously it was considered that the Council had no influence on the time taken to reply to its requests to provide information. Hence little attention was paid to commonly missed items and what could be done to ensure these were reduced.

Risk avoidance actions also made it more difficult to receive clean applications. These messy applications paradoxically increased the risk to the Council of allowing inappropriate development if all issues were not identified.

Articulating these causes of current performance confirmed that progress would only be sustained if change in these areas occurred. Redesign focused on considering each development as a whole from the customer's perspective. The range of work undertaken by each person was maximised to reduce hand-offs from one person to another and increase job satisfaction. The new design for the Building Consents process is represented by *Figure 4* below.

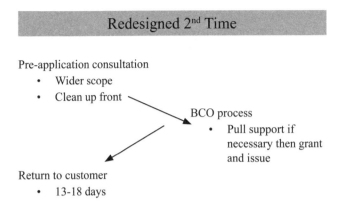

Figure 4: Redesign of Building Consent process

To maximise the range of work undertaken by any one person, effort initially went into encouraging developers and owners to visit the Council before completing their consent application. All relevant staff met with developers to ensure clarity concerning project constraints. This was unsustainable in the long term. However it quickly became obvious that some constraints were routine and predictable.

For instance the Roads Engineer was only interested in visibility at point of access to the road. Hence only intersections and locations where the road curved quickly away from the development site were relevant. Not only did building control officers rapidly recognise which applications they needed support for and call people in for those meetings, but also they found the solutions to the problems were also predictable. They learned what was acceptable in all but exceptional circumstances and, in doing so, became trained to the extent that only a small number of consents required input from specialists.

Interestingly, builders began to understand the Council's requirements and how to minimise cost to their clients. Rather than rely on the Council a number have taken it upon themselves to pass this information on to clients, ensuring greater accuracy in applications.

Resource consent work followed suit, with people in the work being given responsibility for completing consent work end-to-end, supported by technical experts when needed. Understanding of the job and customer satisfaction increased. Timeframes decreased markedly. The following chart of average end-to-end time (see *Figure 5*) highlights the experience for delegated resource consents. Normal end-to-end time in the first half of 2008 was an average of 50 days, with a normal maximum of 122 days. Since undergoing the change this has dropped steadily to around 14 days.

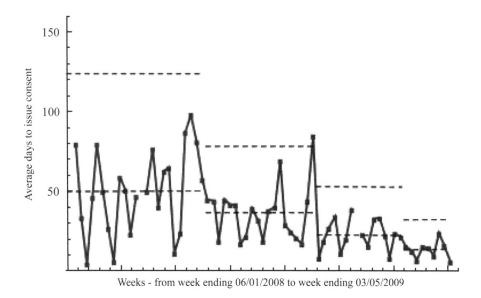

Weeks - from week ending 06/01/2008 to week ending 03/05/2009

Figure 5: Delegated Resource Consents Jan 2008 – May 2009 End-to-End time weekly average

In addition, the average cost of a consent has dropped 13% from $550 in the first half of 2008 to $480 in 2009. FIRs are now down to 15%, from the 70% when the change was initiated. Failure demand has dropped to below 15%.

As one planner remarked:

> *'Before changing I was faced with a barrage of grumpy customers every day. Getting call recognition on my phone made my job much easier as once I could recognise the number of a caller I could decide whether to answer them. If I knew I couldn't give any good news some days I'd let the call go to the answer phone.*

'Now those calls have all but disappeared. If we get one we are interested to know why this is happening. We have the freedom to keep improving, and understanding customer experience is key to that.

'What's even more exciting for me is that I am now mostly involved in real planning work. I am able to use my planning studies and am learning more about the work that really interests me.'[4]

Roads management

Central Otago local roads provide a network of 1850kms servicing an area of 10,000km²; 450kms of sealed roads plus 1000kms of unsealed roads service populated areas of the district; 400kms of tracks provide access to remote farm land and recreational areas in the high country.

Historically the national roads funding authority – now called the New Zealand Transport Agency (NZTA) – had audited CODC operations and Asset Management Plan. Feedback had regularly been that CODC was a good performing council, providing a suitable standard of service from a low cost network[5].

Internally CODC understood it had a poorly functioning relationship between itself, the network consultant and maintenance contractor. Hence there was an interest in applying 'check' (see *Figure 2*). After a review of how work was undertaken, the system picture below (*Figure 6*) was developed:

---

4   Anita Dawe, Planner CODC.

5   Land Transport road assets – Central Otago District, Otago Region. Information as at June 07. LTNZ document benchmarking CODC against all NZ local road authorities for the years 2000-2007. Consistently performing at or above average for sealed road smooth travel conditions while being the second lowest cost per kilometer.

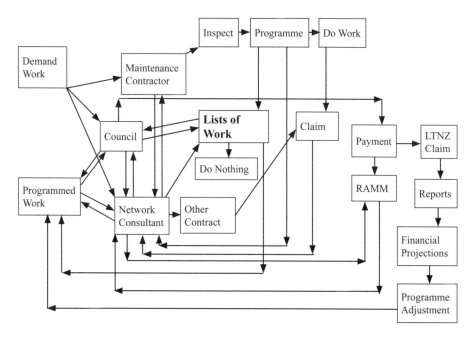

Figure 6: CODC Roads System Picture

Working from left to right it showed that demand entered the system from customers in the form of service requests – and from the program. This was then fed into the three-way contractual relationship between the Council, Maintenance Contractor and Network Consultant. The process was:

1. Work was identified in a monthly program and delivered by the maintenance contractor.

2. Approval of the program was the responsibility of the network consultant; as was ensuring the work was completed before payment claims were authorised.

3. Work that was not able to be carried out was placed on a range of lists awaiting future consideration.

4. With contractors and consultants paid, CODC claimed half of the costs from NZTA.

Initial review of service requests uncovered that 81% of service requests were completed within time despite the high number of hand-offs between organisations shown below:

Service Requests analysed (Total 1688 reviewed over
3-year period 2005-07):

- 42% transferred once
- 13% transferred twice
- 15% three times
- 13% four times
- 8% five times
- 9% more than 5 times

Given that 30% of service requests were transferred to another organisation
four times or more, it seemed incongruous that 81% could be completed on
time. It was discovered that each time the service request was transferred
the time frame was reset. This encouraged transfer of work rather than
completion, especially of those jobs which were difficult or unprofitable
for either the consultant or contractor.

Targets set in contracts for completing service requests were recognised
as the driver for this behaviour. Failure to deal with a service request
within time was an indicator used to determine performance. However
it encouraged poor performance from the customer's perspective as the
contract incentivised people to shift the request rather than complete it.

These targets also contributed to preventable demand in the form of
repeat calls for the same repair work or follow up calls for work not
completed. Analysis of demand showed value calls made up only 34% of
demand, and preventable demand was at least 54%. (The remaining 12%
was not determinable from the information on hand.)

Budgets also influenced programming of work and led to lists of future
work being created from service requests. This enabled requests to be
closed without doing any work. The explanation provided to callers
asking about intentions for the work was 'it's on the list'. In reality this
meant that it was one of 770 items on the future list and unlikely to see
any action for months if not years. Postponed work often worsened into
more expensive jobs in future.

Customer contact was again used to understand the purpose of roads work
and what mattered to customers. These were determined and formulated
as:

Purpose: An efficient, fully accessible, safe roads network.

What matters?

1. Do it once, do it right.
2. Do it before it affects me.
3. Keep me informed.
4. Timeliness.
5. Cost effective / value.

These customer expectations were not being met using the existing management thinking. A review of the creation and implementation of a work program highlighted a troubled process.

Initially inspections were undertaken by the contractor's work supervisors to build a programme based on need. This information was forwarded to the contract manager to build a monthly programme. Manipulation of the proposed work then occurred to ensure profitable work was proposed, as many job types had been tendered at below cost rates. The draft monthly programme was then developed to a value of about one twelfth of the annual budget.

When received by the network consultant the programme was reduced so that any work they considered higher priority could be included, and to ensure a surplus developed in the budget for any unforeseen expenditure. This surplus provided a buffer as any significant over expenditure near year end required reports to be written and potential application to NZTA for budget adjustment. This created the potential risk of not receiving the 50% subsidy for work exceeding approved budgets.

The approved programme was then forwarded to CODC as information, and returned to the contractor for action.

This arrangement had the following consequences:

- Unprofitable work was not programmed, hence the best work for the road often did not drive the work schedule. For instance drainage work along the side of sealed roads had been bid at a low lump sum. Yet drainage work is essential to keep water off roads. With little if any of this work occurring, roads would soon degenerate and need rehabilitation many years before this should otherwise be required. This, and many other works not completed because of low or no margin for the contractor, was increasing the long term cost of maintaining the roads.

- Budget surpluses accumulated during the year were spent in a rush in the last quarter of the year (April to June). In Central Otago winter (the most extreme in New Zealand with minimum temperatures as low as -20°C in mid winter) can arrive any time from mid April onwards. This work was being scheduled at the wrong time, becoming more expensive and less likely to last.

- With the approved programme bearing little resemblance to that initially proposed by supervisors, they lost interest in undertaking thorough inspections and began recording trips to work locations as their inspections. This ad hoc regime meant no comprehensive review of the network was being undertaken.

In summary, the wrong work was being programmed, often at the wrong time, leading to higher costs to maintain the network over time.

It became apparent that the root cause of this situation was the method of tendering for work. Whilst quality was part of the consideration, price significantly influenced who would receive the work. Once price had been driven down, the successful bidder then had little choice but to take whatever actions they could to improve margins so that a profit could be made. The contractors, worried about their profitability, therefore did not tend to focus on the right work to be carried out.

Costs of tendering were reviewed. Over three years the direct cost of letting 27 tenders was $78,000. The addition of supervision costs increased the overall professional services costs to $484,000. On average, nine weeks was required for the tender process alone. Total professional fees were growing, as shown in the table below:

	04/05	05/06	06/07	07/08
Specialist Services	$42	$67	$121	$116
Total fee for year	$475	$547	$611	$626

Figure 7: Professional services cost 2004/05 – 2007/08 ($000)

It became clear that this approach was not only costing almost 10% of the total budget for roads, but also leading to sub-optimal results. Also, non-routine rehabilitation work on the roads was outside the contract with the network consultant, and so drew a further service fee.

Reviewing the claim process further highlighted the incongruity of the existing situation. Each party in the arrangement had reason to manipulate the data for their own purposes. In total, seven separate accounting systems were used to track expenditure.

The claim started with those in the work spending up to an hour a day each morning completing the specified paper work, allocating yesterday's tasks to the appropriate expenditure codes – any one of 120 that then existed. Quantity of work was key for the claim. In addition, control and understanding of actual cost was desirable for the contractor as they needed to understand profitability of work for programming and retendering.

Once in the contractor's office the claim was drawn up from the quantities of work done, relating these back to the programme, contract schedule of rates and indices for escalation. When received by the consultant all claim lines and escalations were checked (a task that took a week a month). Then expenditure was re-coded to codes within available budgets if necessary to avoid reports to CODC and NZTA for variations. CODC would pay any approved contract payment, input expenditure against budget codes in three different systems each for different purposes, and claim the cost-sharing payment from NZTA. This arrangement:

- Provided the Council with false confidence in its budgets and Asset Management Plans.

- Clouded the links between work done and costs as a result of reworking figures multiple times. This meant that when attempts were made to follow these links through from programme to payment it was impossible to do so.

- Resulted in a poor understanding of the actual costs of maintaining the network.

It became clear that the four agencies involved in the work each had different purposes:

1. The maintenance contractor, because of having made an unprofitable bid to win the tender, needed to maintain its margin.

2. The consultant working to a lump sum contract was incentivised to find work outside the contract, minimise their work within the contract and ensure budgets were not overspent.

3. The Council was concerned to ensure that the budget was not overspent, and made this clear to the consultant.

4. Both CODC and NZTA wanted the approved programme to be completed.

These divergent purposes all derived from the contractual relationships that were at the root of the dysfunction between the parties. Excessive and ongoing churn resulted and was exacerbated by a lack of clarity between the parties concerning what a good road looked like. While the tendering process aimed at getting quality at a reasonable price, the long term outcome was increased costs, declining performance of the network and a greater risk to CODC. In response to this new understanding, CODC redesigned its relationship with the parties.

Central to the new arrangement was a unified understanding of what a good road was. With this clarified a simple new flow of work was developed, focusing only on the work of adding value to the roads. Four value steps were identified:

1. Identify the work.
2. Programme the work.
3. Do the work.
4. Pay for the work.

1. Identify the work
There are two methods to identify work needed on the roads. Customers' requests, and inspection to identify roads not at the agreed good road standard. All work needed is recorded in RAMM, an integrated asset management system.

2. Programme the work (doing the right work, at the right time)
A co-ordinated, practical 3-year plus programme with monthly breakdown based on the right time to do the work, and cost estimations based on real cost not unit rates. This provides information for budgets.

3. Doing the work
At the start of each job the right people (especially those who will be onsite doing the work) get together to confirm how the work will be done and what information, if any, the public require. Work then proceeds. If any unpredicted issue arises, those necessary to make a decision are called to the site. Consultants are only engaged when technical expertise

is not available within CODC and the contractor. Road upgrade projects are being delivered as much as 50% below previous cost expectation.

4. Pay for the work

Excessive breakdown of cost centres was removed. The structure of accounts including RAMM recording, for NZTA, the Council and the contractor were mapped, aligned and connected. Information required for payment is now collected when the job is identified. Budget, programme and payments are all integrated. At month end (or daily) a claim can be raised at the push of a button.

Measures designed to record achievement of purpose and comparing spend to budget have been developed. These measures include:

1. Volume of public demand

This data demonstrates our capability to meet the customer's expectation of an efficient, fully accessible and safe road network. This is what matters to them.

- Number of public requests each week from RAMM contractor
- % Value/Failure requests (temporary measure)

2. Time to complete tasks

This measure demonstrates the timeliness of our capability to respond to demand.

- End-to-end time on tasks from RAMM contractor.

3. Achievement of Programme

This measure demonstrates our capability to do work in a cost effective/ value manner, to do it before it affects our customers and to do it once, do it right.

- Work completed to date and backlog of work remaining to date
- % of unplanned work (temporary measure)

4. Revenue and cost information

This demonstrates our capability to identify and provide the funding required to do the work needed to achieve purpose.

- Actual Expenditure against Forecast Expenditure
  Source of data: year to date budget spent compared to budget
  from monthly Council budget sheets.

- Actual funding required for the work against budget.
  Source of data: actual cost of work compared to estimated cost
  from RAMM contractor.

- Budget remaining compared to backlog of work.
  Source of data: monthly budget sheets and RAMM contractor.

Savings of $600,000 have immediately been generated by working
directly with the contractor; this money has been reapplied in the
meantime to rehabilitating the roads.

Service request data could not be compared to the data from before the
change as the previous information was too unreliable to use owing
to multiple service requests for the same job and manipulation of data
within the process.

The reaction of the Roads Manager highlighted the change in approach:

> *'I didn't realise how much of my time was tied up in managing
> the relationship between the consultant and contractor. With
> this now gone and a clearer understanding of what good work
> is, my work is now much more positive and adding value.*

> *'I have the time to get into the work and ensure what we are
> spending our money on the best tasks to make the roads fit for
> users.'* [6]

Management learning

Managers previously concerned themselves with three things. These
were: getting their department's work done, budget control and managing
gaps. This unsuccessful approach operated as follows:

1. Getting work done was achieved by matching activity to staff
   numbers, prioritising work as insufficient resource was available
   to satisfy demand. Unsatisfied demand had become an ongoing
   thorn in the side of the organisation with managers attempting to
   shield workers so they could get on with priority work.

2. Budgets were being controlled by attempting to rein in
   expenditure through the use of specification and tendering of
   external contracts and internal budget tightening. Increasingly,

---

6   Julie Muir Roads Manager CODC.

as budgets had become tighter, over-spends occurred and if they were considered to be the result of manageable influences, deficits had to be made up from future budgets.

3. Gaps between work groups were managed by regular management meetings reporting on activities occurring in each area. These identified jobs which needed cross-department attention and followed up on any friction when these methods failed to achieve integrated work. These approaches tended to be 'after the horse had bolted' and the work was normally aimed at damage control.

Subsequently it was learned that waste, and so the opportunity to reduce cost, was in the flow. As the work design was based on a fragmented, functional design it was the cause of the waste and friction noted above. To emphasise the importance of understanding flow for improvements in cost and performance: no fully analysed flow exhibited more than 10% value steps.

To eliminate this waste in the flow two main approaches were used: minimising hand-offs, and training those in the work against the profile of demand. These actions led to the significant gains in productivity reported above. Not only were customers receiving a more appropriate, timely and cost effective service, but internal frictions began to decrease as better knowledge developed about each department's needs and how these could be addressed. In addition any uncommon demand was seen as a learning opportunity to work together on, rather than just a frustration for one party or another.

Managers now understand that knowledge of predictable demand is the key to managing the work. This enables appropriate training and clarity about when there is a need for those in the work to pull support from others. Predictable failure demand that remains provides focus for both managers and those in the work. They first highlight it then seek to understand why this waste is still being created, and finally design it out.

Clarity about the remaining waste in the flow of work has become the basis for continuous improvement. The attention of managers is shifting from budgets, costs and activity to ensuring a clear understanding of current demand along with knowledge of the remaining waste in the system compared with the redesign ideal.

Managers are learning that information cannot be discovered from being in an office reading reports. Constant attention to what is happening at the interface with the customer is necessary.

Summary

The journey to becoming a systems thinking organisation is not for the fainthearted as it requires a complete overhaul of current organisation practice.

CODC has found that when attention to cost and budget is replaced with attention to flow and waste, costs have declined without the fanfare or upset normally associated with centrally driven change. In place of trying to perform better by satisfying the demand coming through the door, focus has changed to eliminating wasteful work and freeing people to do the work they were employed to do.

Management of risk is replaced by knowledge of risk and systems designed to reduce, if not eliminate, many risks. The result overall has been better performance at a lower cost, with the promise of continuous improvement into the future.

About the author

 John Cooney has been an educator (10 years) and a local authority Chief Executive for over 15 years from 1991, first at Waitaki District Council which unfortunately provided the learning platform for 'what doesn't work in organisational change' and 2002-09 at Central Otago District Council. Currently John is engaged part time by CODC assisting with the ongoing roll-in of work groups to systems thinking.

Central Otago District Council, 1 Dunorling Street, PO Box 122, Alexandra, New Zealand

Tel: (+64) 440-0056   Email: jc@systemsthinking.co.nz

www.codc.govt.nz

CHAPTER 5

ALTERING THE DNA OF AN ORGANISATION: EMBRACING AND EMBEDDING SYSTEMS THINKING

Joanne E McGuigan, Flagship Housing Group Ltd.

This case study illustrates the following:

- The limitations of conventional approaches to raising quality.

- The dangers of government, regulators and managers setting arbitrary targets, which often make performance worse.

- The need to learn about your own assumptions of what is good management. Better results will not be achieved unless your thinking changes.

- The importance of accurate knowledge on how your organisation actually performs from a customer's perspective.

- Obtaining clear data on the reasons for, and the patterns of, customer demand enables innovation.

- The contradiction that when an organisation listens to customers and provides an improved service, they can be penalised by auditors or regulators because arbitrary targets are not met.

- The understanding that many customer demands are linked so that organising employees into functionally specialised departments is nearly always going to provide poor and expensive service.

5. ALTERING THE DNA OF AN ORGANISATION: EMBRACING AND EMBEDDING SYSTEMS THINKING

Joanne E. McGuigan

Background

This case study records the impressive journey of an organisation adopting systems thinking: highlighting the performance improvement realised and the cultural change necessary to sustain such a radical approach.

Flagship Housing Group owns and manages in excess of 20,000 social rented homes across the east of England. We provide a range of housing, maintenance and care services through three subsidiary housing associations: Peddars Way Housing Association, Suffolk Heritage Housing Association and King's Forest Housing. All the associations are not for profit and are regulated by the Housing Corporation with service delivery inspected by the Audit Commission. Flagship Housing Group employs 560 staff; many have been involved in the changes and all share responsibility for ensuring that systems thinking is used in everything we do.

Introduction &and Perspective

> *'We cannot solve our problems with the same thinking we used when we created them'* Albert Einstein

In 2005 Flagship Housing Group started to hear about systems thinking. A number of housing associations and local authorities had started pilot reviews using this methodology and through hearing of these reviews we became curious. We wondered whether systems thinking might offer a better method to drive service improvement across our whole operation. We were not familiar with the works of Deming, Scholtes or Ackoff and had no knowledge of the Toyota Production System or how it might be applied within a service organisation. Indeed we were sceptical about how anything a car company was doing could have a positive impact on a social housing group.

Like many organisations we had sought improvement through a variety of quality tools including Best Value, ISO9000, Charter Mark, Investors in People, Balanced Scorecard, Business Excellence Model and of course a number of ICT-led programmes promising enhanced performance and the usual sector 'best practice' and stretch targets. These traditional improvement methods all worked, to an extent; but the improvements seen were not sustained. We had not succeeded through using these tools in transforming the organisation in the way that we had hoped for, i.e. to be offering a more responsive and adaptive service to our customers and to be stronger than our competitors.

The operating environment within the social housing arena has never been more challenging. Government policy, financial pressures, and social and demographic trends all bring their own complex problems, whilst competition from the private sector and the current public sector 'merger mania', which leads to complex group structures, all add to the pressures felt by many housing associations. In 2003, the Gershon Review examined the scope for efficiencies and developed recommendations to increase the productive time of professionals in the public sector. The recommendations from the Gershon Review alongside the aforementioned internal and external pressures presented a compelling case for our leaders to think differently about how to push service delivery to a new level and genuinely establish competitive edge over the rest of the sector.

Getting started

Flagship Housing Group's senior team commenced a learning programme in the summer of 2005. This programme included reading widely around the work of Deming and his system of profound knowledge, and being introduced to the Toyota Production System and Toyota's culture of organisational learning.

W. Edwards Deming's book *Out of the Crisis* highlighted to us the flaws with command and control leadership, the problems associated with management focus on individual business functions – the 'silo effect' – and the dangers associated with the use of arbitrary targets. We recognised that in our organisation we had developed an expertise in meeting targets which added little or no value to customers. In many cases these targets actually worsened performance from the customer's perspective. Ingenuity was abundant within our organisation – but the creativity was focused on meeting the targets not improving the system.

Toyota's work taught us about identifying the root cause of problems, to understand why the focus of management should be on ensuring clean work in end-to-end flows, and of Toyota's never-ending drive for continuous improvement.

In September 2005 we engaged systems thinking experts Vanguard Consulting to support the team in our learning, and importantly to help us think about how we might begin to bring elements of the Toyota Production System into our service driven organisation.

Through this learning we began to understand that if we wanted to improve performance from the customer's perspective, then we needed to think in a fundamentally different way about the design and management of work (See *Figure 1*). Recognising that our organisation was designed around a traditional command and control style meant that we could understand that our perspective needed to change radically.

Command and control thinking		**System thinking**
Top-down	**perspective**	Outside-in
Functional specialisation	**design**	Demand, value and flow
Separated from work	**decision-making**	Integrated with work
Budget, targets, standards, service levels, activity, etc.	**measures**	Capability versus purpose, variation
Extrinsic (Carrot & stick)	**motivation**	Intrinsic
Manage budgets and people	**ethic**	Act on system

Figure 1: Management Thinking
[Extract from 'Freedom from Command and Control' (2003) by John Seddon]

Leaders across Flagship Housing Group were taught to use a different method for change (*Figure 2*) – a continuous cycle which would truly drive improvement. The change method was later cascaded through the organisation, involving staff from front-line services (Rents, Repairs, Customer Services, Voids teams) to central services (Finance, IT, HR, Health & Safety) and Board Members. Thus the principles of systems thinking and 'Check' became embedded into each staff member's job role; each member of the team being as important to customers as the next, no matter where they 'sat' in the organisation or what role they fulfilled.

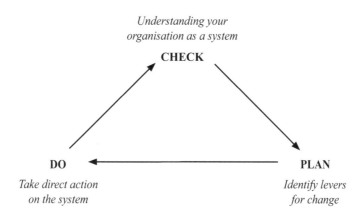

Figure 2: Method for change [Extract from 'Freedom from Command and Control' (2003) by John Seddon.]

The following model (*Figure 3*) was used to perform 'Check' – the part of the change method which helps to identify in a very visual way the issues within a system which affect the way the work works. This in turn affects the capability of the same system to respond to a customer's demand in a way that matters to them.

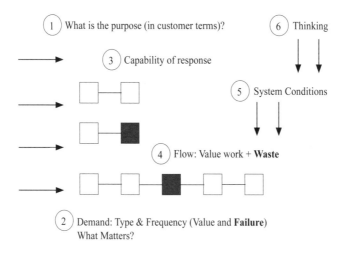

Figure 3: Model for 'Check'
[Extract from 'Freedom from Command and Control' (2003) by John Seddon.]

What was learned

Our systems thinking journey started with a focus on the front line services. By understanding where the demand 'hits' our system, we were able to listen to customers' requests. Broadly speaking, there are 4 main demand service areas for Flagship Housing Group:

- I want a house.
- I want to pay my rent.
- I want/need a repair.
- I want to leave.

In order to understand the system as a whole we engaged staff working up and down the flow of work to create functional group-wide teams to carry out 'Check'. It is this understanding of the work, from end to end, which is critical. Economies come from understanding the flow of work, not from the scale of the service produced, which is the more traditional 'command and control' belief.

Mapping the flow of work enables the waste and value work to be identified. It allows us to see the root causes which are stopping the system from working to meet its purpose. By building a picture of the core steps within the work and interviewing staff at all levels, waste can be highlighted so it can be removed from any redesign. Mapping the flow of work also shows how the thinking of the organisation 'drives' the work. Waste is split into categories:

- Waste that cannot be removed as it is required for the survival of the organisation – this work is kept, but moved to be as far away from delivery of front line service as possible.

- Waste which arises as a result of system conditions – i.e. created by conditions within the process that determine why the service is undertaken in a particular way i.e. structures, measures, procedures, IT Systems. This waste work requires managers to work to change the system conditions (or the way they are perceived) in order to eliminate the waste.

- Waste that can be eliminated simply as a 'quick win'.

Despite meeting all targets (both internal and external) for delivery of a responsive maintenance service, 'Check' revealed that the demand for 'I want a repair' was being met with an appalling level of service. Typically a job (a whole job not just a works order) from the customer's perspective took 125 days to complete. There was a 19% chance that any job raised wouldn't be completed in the same year as it was reported. Repairs often required many visits to the property – a leak under a bath for example could require a plumber, a carpenter, a painter and an inspector (or two) to visit the property. Repairs often did not stay fixed, with components only being replaced as a last resort, instead of doing the right thing at the first point of contact.

We learnt that, in order to drive positive behaviour and increase performance, measures should always be linked to purpose as defined from the customer's perspective. Customers do not care about when an operative turns up to carry out a repair if the job is not done in its entirety. Our customers want us to measure how long it takes to fix a problem from end to end. This is essential for us as an organisation if we are to understand and improve performance.

A complete redesign of the responsive maintenance system resulted in outstanding performance improvements. Jobs are now completed predictably within 0-12 days, with an average across the Group of 8.6 days. Understanding the end-to-end works required and working with contractors to multi-skill operatives has resulted in 83% of jobs being carried out with a single visit to the property. Empowering the expert (the person who carries out the job) to make the right decisions and understanding that it is more cost effective to do the right thing the first time ensures that now 97% of repairs effected stay fixed. The effect of getting it 'right first time' has been that the demand on the responsive repairs service has reduced by 25%.

Other improvements seen across Flagship Housing Group since we adopted systems thinking include:

- Failure demand (demand caused by a failure to do something or do something right for the customer) has reduced from 70% to 30%.

- Voids (empty properties) are re-let quicker, with 80% of properties relet within one week (down from an average of 4 weeks).

- 30% of voids are re-let back to back (within one day) – this was not achieved in the old system.

- Overall maintenance costs have reduced to September 2003 levels.

- Gross rent arrears have reduced by more than £500k.

- Printing, postage, stationery and office-running costs have also been reduced to September 2003 levels.

Example of innovation

The most recent review that Flagship Housing Group undertook looked at the mechanism provided for customers to contact us. Historical working practices and preferences of individuals dictated that we had two call centres providing a service to customers during usual office hours of 0900-1700hrs Monday-Friday. If customers wanted to contact us outside these hours then, if it was an emergency, this could be done by telephoning Assist & Assure – Flagship Housing Group's alarm company. Customers were invariably handed off to others in the organisation, which in itself resulted in an increase in failure demand.

When looking at the data for this service, it was found that each day 60-100 customers were predictably trying to call Flagship Housing Group outside office hours, with the majority not electing to leave a message or go through to the emergency lines available. Of the customers who did elect to call the emergency telephone number, 50% of calls were not, from Flagship's perspective, deemed to be an emergency and so callers were invariably advised to call again the next working day during office hours. The system was clearly unfit for purpose.

The redesign of this service has resulted in the opening of a 24/7 service – Flagship Response. Launched in May 2009, customers of Flagship Housing Group can now call Flagship Response 365 days a year and their enquiry will be dealt with. The ethos of Flagship Response is that the telephone transaction is as important as the face-to-face transaction. Training based on a thorough understanding of all customer demands ensures that Flagship Response staff are equipped to answer all queries any time of day or night.

This training ensures that 83% of demands which can be dealt with in-house are done so, meaning that customers go away with an answer. This eliminates further failure demand – which has dropped from 30% to 8%. Demands received at times when previously we were closed now account for 20% of all calls to Flagship Response. Customers can and do call in the middle of the night to pay rent or report a repair. Monday mornings, once the busiest time of the week, are now quieter due to eliminating the 'pent up' demand which arose from customers saving up demands from 1700 hours on the preceding Friday. This makes resource planning easier as, though peaks and troughs in demand still remain, the range of predictable levels of demand is tighter.

Flagship Response acts as a hub for continuous improvement for Flagship Housing Group. In an effort to ensure that we are providing good quality of service today, Flagship Response captures all demand received. Filtering this data by type of demand (value or failure plus reason for failure) allows us, with good knowledge of the frequency of demand, to feed this important information through to other parts of the organisation. This information, which tells us about the capability of systems to respond to demands, is displayed on capability charts which are used because they help managers to ask different and better questions about the management of work. This in turn leads to the improvement of systems. Managers inform Flagship Response about changes made to the system and the effect of changes can be measured to understand the impact of the changes on the customer's experience.

Flagship Housing Group is keen to ensure that it is a dynamic organisation, reacting to the needs of its customers and shaping the way for future services based on the demands it receives. Flagship Response aims to ensure we are providing this quality of service tomorrow by capturing currently unmet demands (the things we say 'no' to) and using this information to inform the strategies of years to come.

Improvements seen have all been realised through taking a whole system approach. This approach allows the identification of considerable amounts of waste caused by organisational design which in turn offers huge scope for continuous improvement and provides an opportunity to redesign systems from a customer's point of view. Once systems have been redesigned and (previously wasted) capacity has become realised, this capacity can be utilised to do more value work for customers.

Regulation and Inspection

We are aware that systems thinking challenges almost all conventional notions about the use of performance indicators, service standards and targets. In an environment such as ours, where regulation is undertaken by inspectors (who are not in the flow of work) who pay close attention to numbers and an assessment of an organisation's ability to publish and adhere to service standards, it was very important to make every effort to convince regulatory bodies and inspectors that we are doing the 'right thing'.

The Key Lines of Enquiry used by the Audit Commission when assessing performance of Housing Associations are, at first sight, not dissimilar to our strategic aims as an organisation – indeed they detail the excellence that we strive for. The place for discussion is not around the broad themes of the Key Lines of Enquiry, but in how performance is assessed against them. Our experience is that Key Performance Indicators (KPI) and traditional targets drive the wrong behaviours in the work. They do not serve to help people in the work to focus on what is important to the customer but instead encourage a focus on making the numbers. Targets, in our experience, were having a negative impact rather than achieving the improvement they were seeking.

A classic example of targets driving the wrong behaviour can be seen again using the example of the demand 'I want a repair'. Our customers want repairs done when *they* want them done. Restrictions imposed by regulators often conflicted with the wishes of our customers and so led to us being penalised for not meeting prescribed timescales if we attended when customers asked us to. In order to maintain our perceived standards, staff would cancel jobs and re-raise them closer to the date when the work was being carried out. Had this not been done, we would have found ourselves in the situation whereby we were providing an excellent service which looked 'bad' against KPIs.

Other imposed targets included categorising repairs as 'emergency', 'non emergency' and 'routine'. In reality, when viewed from a customer's perspective, meeting this target meant that it was acceptable to board up a window which had been broken and 'tick the box' – because doing so met the target. Much better is the new measure which, though typically taking longer, is a true reflection of the whole customer experience rather than a portion of it. In the past, our traditional command and control management thinking ensured that managers paid close attention to these KPIs without realising the detriment they were causing to service provision. When one realises that KPIs are used as a guide to determine funding, the reasons behind managers striving to evade penalisation are obvious.

Whilst Flagship Housing Group does collect data to ensure that we satisfy the needs of the regulatory bodies, we do not use this data to demonstrably improve performance day-to-day as we believe the indicators to be of little or no value to the customer. We regard this specific data collection work as a 'tax' that must be paid, and we continue to work to persuade inspectors of the reasons why such measurement of performance should change. In order to drive our day-to-day performance we use new measures and data which allow us to understand what the purpose of the system is from the customer's perspective and then measure our ability to deliver on that purpose in a way that our customers want us to. This gives us a unique insight into what is actually going on in the work (especially from the customer's point of view) and does help to drive improvement on the ground. Thus, rather than 'fiddling the figures to meet the targets', systems thinking relies on making intelligent use of its intelligent work force to meet each customer's nominal value (the way they want their service delivered). We have learnt that allowing the customers to establish their own nominal value does not result in ridiculous timescales being set or unrealistic demands being placed. In fact our customers are reasonable and rational people – just like us!

Over the past 2 years, Flagship Housing Group has regularly met with regulators and inspectors, in addition to working with the Chartered Institute of Housing, the industry's professional body, in order to showcase its learning. Whilst Flagship Housing Group recognises that some more traditional organisations may applaud the sharing of 'best practice methods', we are actively seeking to change this viewpoint and instead encourage the sharing of learning and principles of work, not method.

We know from experience that everything we need to improve our organisation is within our own organisation, not in someone else's organisation. The Chartered Institute of Housing have recently recognised our innovative and flexible approach to responsive repairs and voids and, through published guides of their own, have recognised that our learning and working principles ought to be held up as exemplary within the housing sector.

Resilience is key – embedding systems thinking

We had learnt that resilience is the key to success and that if the decision was made for Flagship Housing Group to start using systems thinking as a methodology, it must not be optional for anyone. Early on in our journey, a strong message was given to staff. The message was that whilst we were seeking improvement in service (through efficiency of flow) through a new methodology, this was not a redundancy exercise. The message was delivered from the Chief Executive of the organisation and it was made clear that there would be a job for everyone who was willing to adopt systems thinking as a way of working. Their job would change and we couldn't guarantee (at that time) what the new jobs would be, but staff willing to change their methods and learn would be supported through the changes. Few staff left the organisation as the majority recognised the need for something different.

The Flagship Service System was designed to aid staff in their quest to keep using systems thinking every day to help us in our pitch for perfection. The following set of guiding principles is designed into every staff member's job description and outlines the behaviour which Flagship Housing Group expects staff to demonstrate:

- **Do what matters to our customers**
  This means that we understand what matters to each and every individual customer in the way that we deliver our services. It's about treating customers as individuals rather than imposing the standards of others on them.

- **Get it right at first point of contact**
  This guiding principle is about empowering front line staff to take decisions and deliver services that will meet the demands of the customer.

- **Only do the value work**
  Our systems are designed to incorporate only the 'value' work in a process. This increases efficiency through eliminating waste and therefore increases our capacity to do more for our customers.

- **Minimise hand-offs**
  We know from experience that problems are more likely to occur when work is passed to others or 'handed off' between staff. We also understand that our customers prefer to deal with as few people as possible. We design our work and empower our people to minimise hand-offs and therefore reduce the possibility of problems occurring.

- **Minimise waste**
  In looking at the work we do from a customer's perspective, we have learned to see significant waste caused by organisational design. We try to strip out this waste from our processes, removing it completely where possible and, if this isn't possible, we move it out of the way of the staff who deliver services to customers.

- **Do clean work in end-to-end flows**
  By seeing the whole organisation as a system and stopping working in 'silos' we can improve the effectiveness of our work. Managers, staff and partners work in end-to-end flows rather than just working on 'their bit'.

- **Design against demand**
  By understanding the nature of demand coming into Flagship Housing Group, we design our work to best meet the needs of our customers. We understand that the nature of demand changes and that our systems need to be flexible to adapt to these changes.

The nature of the design of the Group structure is that services such as IT, Finance and Human Resources are managed centrally, delivering services to each of the Housing Associations. Fundamental to the success of embedding systems thinking was the understanding that central services also exist to serve the customer and the breaking down of previous notions about 'internal customers'. Staff from central services were included when 'Check' was carried out in the front line – this allowed learning about the impact on the customer of a team of staff who are remote in terms of work flow.

Reorganising the business to meet demands

After using systems thinking to review front line services it became apparent that the staffing structure was a major systems condition hindering the flow of work. 'Check' was applied to the staffing structure. Gathering data about type and frequency of demand, asking people who were involved in the work about how they thought the organisation should be designed and asking customers 'what mattered to them' when contacting us was vital. A redesign was proposed – it moved the organisation of work away from the functional specialism that we had created (and thought essential) and towards more generic roles based purely on customer demand.

Understanding that most demands were linked was the greatest driver for creating generic roles – for example 'I want a house' must be linked to 'I want to leave' as properties must become void (empty) prior to us granting a new tenancy to a new customer. Likewise 'I want to pay rent': the payment (or non payment in some cases) of which is linked to 'I want a repair'. Customers told us that they wanted to speak to one person who could deal with the majority of their problems, that they wanted to build a relationship with that one person and they wanted that person to do whatever was necessary to solve all their problems.

In order to address this need we designed 'Community Manager' roles, based in the field, to look after all demands (and administration work around those demands) from a specific geographical area of houses. In having a thorough understanding of the type and frequency of demand, Flagship Housing Group is able to ensure that the 'patches' of properties were sized according to the number and variety of demands. The smallest 'patch' area covers 80 properties and the demands from these properties are looked after by one Community Manager. Other 'patches' range in size from 200-800 properties, all according to how many demands a Community Manager can, predictably, cope with. By empowering the Community Managers to do whatever it takes to meet the customers' demands, we are ensuring that customers are not passed from pillar to post but are receiving a true end-to-end service. This means that there are no longer any administrative posts within Flagship, and the only support roles are the support services such as finance, HR and IT, which have the job of supporting front line staff to do whatever it takes to meet the demands of customers.

Senior managers are learning to see the organisation as a system. In so doing, they understand that variation in performance is due to the system (Deming said that 95% variation in performance is due to the system and 5% to the individual). With fewer managers in the hierarchy (the reorganisation saw a move from nine levels of management to just three), the role of a manager becomes of a higher value when viewed from the customer's perspective.

Leading systems thinking in a service organisation like Flagship means managers being in the actual work. They must not be 'hands off', behind a desk, trading opinions, always in meetings, doing one-to-one appraisals with staff setting targets they will never achieve, or networking, benchmarking best practice and so on. They must be 'hands on', looking at capability measures, basing decisions on good knowledge and data rather than opinion, designing our service response on real demand, and most critically, understanding and delivering 'what matters to our customers'.

In order to achieve this, each Community Manager is assigned to an Area Manager. The Area Managers each have approximately 10 Community Managers reporting to them. The job of all Area Managers is to 'Act on the System'. This entails managers working in the flow of work – unblocking blockages so staff can add value to our customers and working on the causes of cost and on eliminating waste from the system. This means being visionary and understanding what it is that gets in the way of doing a good job. Managers ask questions including:

- How do you know you're doing a good job?

- Show me your measures.

- What have you done (to the system) to get these performance measures?

- What are you going to do tomorrow (to the system) to improve on performance?

- *And most importantly*: What can I do to help you improve the system?

Managers work up and down the flow, within Flagship Housing Group and also with partners. Our work in the past years has highlighted the need to work more closely with contractors and other partners – after all, from the customer's perspective it's all the same system.

Managers work from wherever their flow takes them – be that our offices or the offices of partners. Managers are continually working with contractors in their flows, identifying and removing blockages whilst helping our partners to also adopt systems thinking principles. Through their spending time in the flow and asking the experts (the people who do the work) what needs to be done to help them provide the service, we are ensuring that managers' time is predominantly spent on value work. Working this way, using data every day and understanding what happens within the flow of work gives managers real control – not the illusion of control which we had before. This new way of working also eliminates the need for formal one-to-ones, which we found were only previously required due to managers' inability to communicate regularly with staff.

Board members at Flagship Housing Group are very supportive of systems thinking. It became apparent that the challenges and complexities of a Group structure meant that there was much bureaucracy and a lot of paperwork (most of which was duplicated) surrounding the servicing of four Boards and five Committees which were established prior to introducing systems thinking. Board members themselves suggested and were instrumental in a complete review of corporate governance using systems thinking. Findings of members revealed a lack of clarity around the roles and purpose of the boards: that on average 72% of a Board meeting was spent discussing operational issues or statutory returns, whilst only 9% of time was spent understanding performance. 96% of the time when a decision was required it was the same as the decision recommended by managers.

Boards now meet more regularly and have clearly defined purposes. A customer board has been established, made up entirely of residents who focus on strategic issues. Board members spend time working in the flow, from listening to demands coming in to Flagship Response, to visiting customers with tradesmen, and understanding what the data is saying about our capability to respond. Managers are responsive to what matters to Board members, therefore it is imperative that Board members are paying attention to the right things. Board members identify blockages in order to help improve the service further and remain keen advocates of systems thinking.

Looking ahead

Systems thinking has transformed Flagship Housing Group into a progressive, modern organisation which applauds innovation and is on the way to establishing a culture of continual learning and improvement. Layers of management have been reduced and restructured management teams are continuing to discover and develop their roles within a systems thinking organisation. Increased numbers of front line staff are not just empowered but expected to make decisions (they – not the managers – are the experts), and the innovative and creative thinking of individuals is harnessed to ensure we are meeting demands and solving problems, not meeting targets. Change and improvement is continuous: the stance which Flagship Housing Group has adopted is that it is absolutely better to be doing 'the right thing *righter*', with good measures and data, than continuing to do the wrong thing whilst procrastinating about what change might look like.

About the author

 Joanne E. McGuigan is Head of Customer Excellence at Flagship Housing Group Ltd. She is the lead in systems thinking for this Group of Housing Associations and is personally respected and consulted by others looking to undertake similar service improvement programmes within the public sector.

Joanne started her career in the world of housing in 1999, working as a Property Manager for a private organisation in London. In 2004 she moved to Suffolk, joining Flagship Housing Group. Joanne progressed to her current post as Head of Customer Excellence in 2006 and has been leading significant learning group-wide since then. She implemented systems thinking through which the Group has started to achieve very impressive results. Joanne is also responsible for launching Flagship Response, the UK's first 24/7 call centre for housing, having taken the project from initial concept through to successful implementation and management.

Flagship Housing Group Ltd, Keswick Hall, Norwich, Norfolk, NR4 6TJ

Tel. 01603 255400   Email: Joanne.mcguigan@flagship-housing.co.uk

CHAPTER 6

TRANSFORMING GLASGOW HOUSING ASSOCIATION: COMMON SYSTEM, COMMON SENSE

Graeme Hamilton, Glasgow Housing Association

This case study illustrates the following:

- The value of an objective analysis of an organisation's current performance.

- The need to explicitly determine the purpose of the organisation. Why does it exist? To find out if perceived purpose is the same as practised purpose.

- It is vital to analyse demand. A service cannot be effectively designed to meet demand unless demand is understood.

- The power of identifying waste by charting the flow of work end-to-end through the entire system.

- Experiments that allow solutions to emerge are more effective than plans without knowledge, as a way to improve an organisation.

- People only understand systems thinking when they do the analysis of demand and waste for themselves.

6. Transforming Glasgow Housing Association: Common System, Common Sense

Graeme Hamilton, Glasgow Housing Association

Background

Glasgow Housing Association (GHA) owns and manages, through a network of local housing associations, 73,000 socially rented homes across the whole of Glasgow. GHA is the largest social housing landlord in the United Kingdom. The association is a not for profit, tenant-led organisation, regulated by the Scottish Housing Regulator. The GHA Board, which is the main decision-making body of the association, is comprised of 15 members, 6 tenants, 4 independent members, 4 Glasgow City Councillors and the GHA Chief executive. The Chair of the Board is a GHA tenant.

In September 2007, the GHA was inspected by the Scottish Housing Regulator, known at that time as Communities Scotland. The inspection was thorough and intense, focusing on all aspects of the housing association's business, including rent management, repairs and maintenance, house letting, governance, learning and development and investment. GHA was only awarded a 'C' grading. The detailed report highlighted many failings and weaknesses across the organisation, resulting in a 60 point Improvement Plan. It specifically noted that our 'performance in collecting rent is poor and worsening'.

GHA has been the focus of much political discussion in the six years of its existence. It was born from a need to give tenants more control in the management of their homes. It developed through various models, to be strongly promoted by the Scottish Executive as a transitional vehicle towards community ownership. GHA grew up amidst dissent about how best to split the large organisation up whilst adhering to all the budgetary and business plan caveats that had been put in place. It was lately retained as one organisation that will fulfil most of the wider housing and regeneration needs of Glasgow. It will work where required in solid partnership with Glasgow City Council and other organisations. One of GHA's biggest failings was in not listening to, or meeting all the needs of our customers. This was evidenced by the Scottish Housing Regulator in September 2007.

A new role – Director of Housing and Customer Services – was formed, replacing the Director of Housing Services who left in September 2007. The new Director, Martin Armstrong, had experienced the huge change for the benefit of customers that had been derived from systems thinking in West Lothian Council. Therefore Vanguard Scotland were engaged to assist GHA in applying systems thinking to bring about the improvements identified as necessary by the recent inspection. The results from systems thinking in the first 12 months (2008-09) are that service has improved, costs have fallen, income has risen and staff morale is higher.

What is systems thinking?

Systems thinking is derived from the principles of management that were employed in Toyota car production – a manufacturing organisation from the 1950s onwards. Toyota, like many of the Japanese manufacturing companies, benefited from the philosophy expounded by W. Edwards Deming, who worked in Japan after the Second World War and supported the newly emerging economy.

Deming (1982) criticised many organisations for their belief in command and control by managers, short-term thinking, management focus on functional silo operations and the use of arbitrary targets. It was to be some 30 years before the American car industry changed their philosophy to match that of Japan.

With its roots firmly in manufacturing and production, it wasn't immediately apparent that these ideas could also be applied to the service sector. Only recently have managers realised how the principles of continuous improvement, reducing waste and costs and improving business systems could be used in the service sector.

John Seddon (2005) identified the potential to help service sector businesses achieve significant improvement in performance and quality of customer service by adopting Deming's principles. Seddon adapted and updated Deming's Plan, Do, Check, Act (PDCA) Cycle. Seddon recognised that before you plan what changes to bring about, you need to first 'Check' what is currently happening in the business. Therefore, although it remains a continuous cycle, the starting point is different from Deming's.

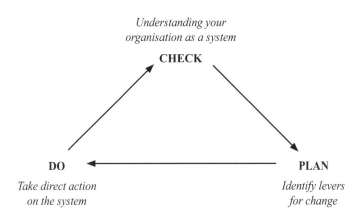

Figure 1: Method for change [Extract from 'Freedom from Command and Control' (2003) by John Seddon.]

The next section describes how the Glasgow Housing Association has used this model. It details the method used to bring about continuous improvement in the delivery of a quality housing service to our customers over the past 12 months.

What we used to do in the Glasgow Housing Association

GHA, like most Registered Social Landlords (RSLs) in Scotland, was a traditional target-driven, top-down management organisation, heavily regulated with monthly reports provided both internally and to our funders, Board and Regulator. Regardless of the level of shouting, and the high number of exception reports that were demanded and laboriously produced, performance improvements were limited. Generally, where teams improved and sustained that improvement against target, there was no incentive to strive further as the target had been beaten and everyone could then 'coast' along until they once more fell below target. Target setting took up many hours for all managers. They were then obliged to divide their office target amongst staff, even when it was absolutely apparent that many of the targets would never be achieved.

Key data on our core business areas at the start of 2008-09 financial year:

- Rent arrears stood at £10.1m.

- End-to-end relet times for all empty properties were averaging 56 days.

- We were only letting 49% of our houses within four weeks.

In summary our performance was not good and, by and large, was not improving. Benchmarking against other RSLs showed that we were well short of the mark in Scotland, and this was also demonstrated in the findings from the Regulatory inspection. Further evidence of our poor performance over the preceding two years is shown below:

- During financial years 2006-07 and 2007-08 there were over 20,000 refusals on our properties, each representing wasted time, effort, visits and phone calls from our staff and potential customers.

- Nearly 1 in 5 of our new tenancies to customers who were on the waiting list or who were homeless failed within 12 months.

- After analysis, we found we were generating 80% failure demand from our customers.

Senior managers decided to review three core processes using two consultants. Teams of front line housing staff with the required business area knowledge and experience were brought in to review these processes – collecting rents, letting houses, carrying out repairs and maintenance, and implementing investment programmes. This was a fast and furious experience for these teams, as their roles were not back-filled and were therefore being covered by colleagues.

Purpose

The first stage was to determine exactly what the purpose of the organisation was. Many within the teams decided that the purpose of GHA was to collect rent. As the teams then worked through the evidence, it became apparent that we did very little to do that – we told the tenant at sign-up stage what the rent would be and we issued them with a rent card. Our efforts were almost exclusively then focused on chasing up rent arrears.

- We monitored non-payment of rents every 4 weeks.

- We wrote thousands of letters advising tenants that they had not paid their rent and asking them to come and see us.

- We instigated court proceedings after 28 days, on an IT system that generated automatic arrears letters if no payment had been made in that time.

- We made and re-made many arrangements to clear former tenant debt; we took no, or little, cognisance of the delays in the housing benefit system (which often meant that that financial transfer didn't happen within the 28 days); we didn't counsel the tenants on whether they could afford the rent on the house they had been selected for.

- We didn't discuss how, where or when the tenant would pay nor what to do if they experienced difficulty.

- We certainly didn't seek any payment in advance or upfront at the start of a tenancy.

Our perceived purpose (collecting rent) was completely at odds with our practised purpose (chasing arrears).

Another example: our repairs contractor regularly presented a monthly report which showed that 99% of all jobs were completed within the target timescale. As the team worked through the data it became apparent that to meet the target, jobs that were not completed but nearly at their time limit were being signed off as finished. A common reason for the 'sign off' would be: 'No Access to property possible', and then paperwork for a 'new' job was raised, so resetting the clock for the target. Each job created attracted a cost to the GHA and each one represented an increased waiting time for the tenant to get the job completed to satisfaction. However, the reports used showed that the contractor was meeting the targets set, i.e. the job was signed off within the target number of days. In summary, GHA had spent tens of thousands of pounds unnecessarily because of the focus on the wrong targets and our customers were not receiving the best possible service from our contractor.

Customer experience

The front line teams then considered the experience of the service from a customer's point of view. Taking again an example from Repairs: the group members set up a demand analysis in their own offices of the telephone calls and counter enquiries on repair issues. The group also monitored demand at one of the contractor's service centres and at the call centre run by the contractor.

Demand analysis is one of the elements used in systems thinking to gather data upon which to make informed decisions about improving service. There are two types of demand: value – which is desirable as it demonstrates you are providing the type of service that your customers positively wish to 'pull' from you – and failure – which you need to know about in order to develop actions to remove it. Examples of failure demand would be tenants chasing up the completion of a repair, asking when the work is to be done or complaining that the work has not been completed to an acceptable standard.

The analysis of the demand showed that there was a huge amount of failure in the system. Staff were not looking at previous repairs and had no understanding of warranty periods – they simply created a new job as quickly as possible to get the customer off the phone. The findings of this particular review shaped the tone, content and emphasis of the tender document for the new Repairs contract which was to start in April 2009.

Refusal of offers of a house

An analysis of the reasons why prospective tenants in 2006-08 refused the offer of a house showed that 44% were caused by the tenant failing to attend or cancelling a viewing. Most of the remainder were because of the location or concerns about the property. Most of these issues could have been avoided with more detailed and informed discussion when the applicant first expressed interest in securing a tenancy. Staff would then have been better able to ensure that offers of properties more closely matched those that the tenants would be interested in seeing. We also needed to review our communication methods to ensure that prospective tenants were being given the right information in good time in an effective way, to ensure they turned up at the property.

Following this, in the first quarter of 2009-10, after the interventions in all our Local Housing Organisations (LHO), the numbers in the 'Failed to attend a house viewing' category fell from 44% to 27% of the total reasons for rejecting an offered property. We are steadily moving in the right direction but we recognise it will take time for many experiments to be started and for change in all areas to be implemented. To further reduce waste in the system we will focus on improving the quality of early discussions with customers who wish to take on a tenancy.

System Pictures

Having gathered and analysed demand, the groups then set about building a systems picture, i.e. a visual depiction of the stages of each process. For example, the Letting Group looked at what happened from the moment someone arrived at a local office, advising they were giving up their tenancy, all the way through to the next new tenant moving in. At each stage waste and impact on individuals and the organisation were captured. This involved the group members 'walking the journey' of that particular process to identify what really happened.

An example of the waste found was the process that was typically followed when a tenant wished to leave their property. The tenant was greeted by a receptionist in the office and their name taken and recorded. The tenant took a seat and waited for a Housing Assistant to become free. They were then interviewed and asked to fill in a form. The tenant left after being informed they had to hand in their keys no more than 28 days later.

A Housing Assistant then took the form and left it in a basket on a Housing Officer's desk. Two days later the Housing Officer input the 'give-up' details into the IT system. Because the question wasn't asked by the Housing Assistant, the Housing Officer then had to contact the tenant to check if they would be agreeable to having other people view the house before they moved out. Also, because no financial check was made, the Finance Officer then contacted the tenant to discuss arrangements to clear any outstanding debts. And so on.

Systems thinking encourages managers to look at these pictures in order to identify the waste, the impact on staff and other resources and the customer service provided. So, in our example above, if the Housing Assistant had a checklist she would know to check the rent accounts, make arrangements to clear any debt, agree that early accompanied views may be carried out and arrange a suitable date and time for the Housing Officer to complete the end of tenancy inspection.

Figure 2 below provides one example of a current system picture for one Local Housing Organisation (LHO), in this case from a prospective tenant submitting an application for housing to receiving confirmation of that application being set up. *Figure 2* shows the processes and steps required for this part of the letting process to be completed, and it lists the waste found.

Managers are often astounded when they produce these pictures after mapping the flow and gathering the evidence. The waste generated is more than they could have imagined. Feedback to the team on the whole range of their findings is often put across in a passionate but balanced way. Managers quickly recognise that our business systems have been causing staff to do things in a certain way. The meetings are often very fruitful and start to embed the wider buy-in from staff to bringing about change to their working practices, based on what a perfect system would look like from a customer's perspective.

GHA ~ Housing Applications

APPLICATION RECEIVED AT COUNTER	APPLICATION RECEIVED IN MAIL	PASSED TO FINANCE TEAM FOR DEBT CHECK	PASSED BACK TO ALLOCATIONS TEAM	LETTER SENT ADVISING OF POINTS/ PRIORITY
If no proof for main applicant, form given back	If no proof, write out (twice) to applicant	Access to IFS?	Assistants load waiting list and pass back to housing officer for checking (points totals etc.)	Letter does not say anything about existing debts
No proof requested for others on application	Unloaded applications filed in main files (so no record of what is loaded or not)		For transfers, housing officer checks effective date and loads application	
No check done at reception for duplicate applications				
Nothing done one stop				
No discussions re affordability				

Figure 2: System picture – showing waste

Having now identified exactly what is happening in each process, the groups set about determining what a perfect process from the customer's point of view would look like. The outcome was a 'perfect' system picture (*Figure 3*). We recognised that some steps may not yet have been removed because of legislation, or because our IT systems needed to be changed. The process of continuous improvement (Check, Plan, Do) and occasional further demand analyses would allow us to regularly re-focus and make necessary changes in the stages.

In parallel with this work inside GHA, some of the teams also carried out a two-week intervention in Glasgow City Council. Many of our processes overlap with their processes (letting houses to homeless applicants or collecting housing benefit to pay rent being two key examples). It was essential therefore to engage with partners in Council departments so that the end-to-end experience for the customer was seamless as processes passed across and between the two organisations.

Having finally designed system perfect, it was time to present to the Director and secure an agreement to embark on an implementation of the required change programme across the whole organisation (and where necessary in Glasgow City Council too, with their Directors' agreement) at the earliest possible opportunity.

The picture below provides a flavour of the diagrams that managers shared with their staff in developing an appreciation of the issues identified through an end-to-end review of the processes. This example is a perfect picture of what GHA aspires to achieve through the review of the letting process. Having gone through the pain of an intervention for themselves, managers and staff are more attuned to bringing about change. The over-arching work that was done at the start of the whole review aided in the development of a consistent perfect process that would, and should, apply in each and every business location.

In developing their experiments, LHO staff are able to consider what actions are needed to move from where they are to where the organisation believes all LHOs should consistently be.

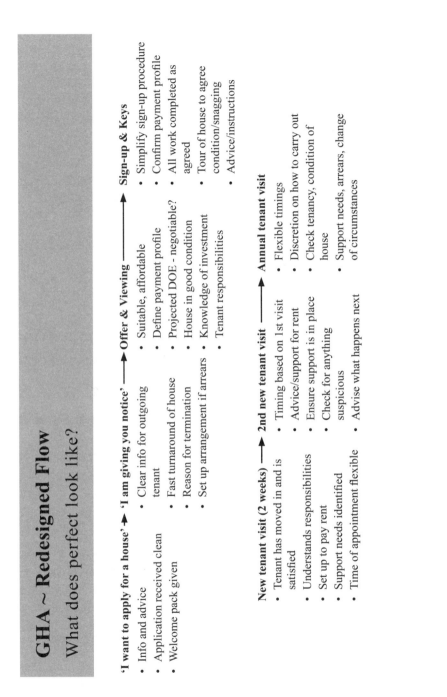

GHA ~ Redesigned Flow

What does perfect look like?

'I want to apply for a house' → **'I am giving you notice'** → **Offer & Viewing** → **Sign-up & Keys**

'I want to apply for a house'
- Info and advice
- Application received clean
- Welcome pack given

'I am giving you notice'
- Clear info for outgoing tenant
- Fast turnaround of house
- Reason for termination
- Set up arrangement if arrears

Offer & Viewing
- Suitable, affordable
- Define payment profile
- Projected DOE - negotiable?
- House in good condition
- Knowledge of investment
- Tenant responsibilities

Sign-up & Keys
- Simplify sign-up procedure
- Confirm payment profile
- All work completed as agreed
- Tour of house to agree condition/snagging
- Advice/instructions

New tenant visit (2 weeks) → **2nd new tenant visit** → **Annual tenant visit**

New tenant visit (2 weeks)
- Tenant has moved in and is satisfied
- Understands responsibilities
- Set up to pay rent
- Support needs identified
- Time of appointment flexible

2nd new tenant visit
- Timing based on 1st visit
- Advice/support for rent
- Ensure support is in place
- Check for anything suspicious
- Advise what happens next

Annual tenant visit
- Flexible timings
- Discretion on how to carry out
- Check tenancy, condition of house
- Support needs, arrears, change of circumstances

Figure 3: Perfect Solution

How the changes were carried out

We now knew how imperfect many of our core business systems were. We also were aware of the negative impact of repeat and chase up calls on our customers. These also were causing our staff to be frustrated, annoyed and reduced their capacity to focus on value work.

In June 2008 we ran a series of 6 workshops (one per shared service geographical grouping) to alert front-line staff to the key findings of these recent reviews and to prepare them for the roll out of system perfect solutions. This was also a chance to validate our findings amongst all front-line service staff.

At this time a further four managers were seconded to form a core team of seven to work up and deliver the solutions identified for a redesign of the whole business system. The roll out of the solutions became a project in its own right. The team also would be required to facilitate the change programme in each of 45 Local Housing Organisations (LHOs).

Each secondee was responsible for different business areas within the broad heading of 'Rents and Letting'. Improvements in Repairs and Capital Works were implemented elsewhere. The team built many new solutions, a number of which had been previous good practice which had withered away over the years.

For example, our whole emphasis was now on ensuring that a prospective tenant had all the information, knowledge and support up front in order to be able to sustain a tenancy and to know how much rent to pay, when and where to pay it, and that it was affordable. Our guidance and procedure notes for staff changed and a training/briefing programme developed, called simply 'The Rents and Letting Guide'.

We reviewed all our standard letters, deleting about 90% of them immediately and replacing them with templates that required staff to populate them with appropriate customer specific information. We ensured that staff would discuss rent and affordability at every interaction with a customer or prospective customer – at application stage, at accompanied viewing, at sign-up, at move in, at new tenant visit stage and at every other contact during their tenancy.

Together with staff from Glasgow City Council Revenue and Benefits and from the Homeless Partnership, we developed improved practices. For example, we set up a pilot scheme called the 'Verification Framework' where GHA staff verify the identification documents produced by the tenant, scan them and send them to the Benefit Centre. We are still re-designing our sign-up pack to make it more streamlined and beneficial to our new tenants. We are currently looking at targeted variation of the packs for transferring tenants who may not need the whole package that new tenants to GHA would require.

The effect of GHA's Court criteria 2007-08

Recognising that chasing arrears was not the purpose of the business and that the process generated huge amounts of waste for very little return, we reviewed our court criteria.

Tenants in arrears	=	23,000
1st Reminders	=	12,816
Final Reminders	=	6258
Average times at court	=	3.5
[Maximum times at court	=	7]
Decrees granted	=	962 (15% of total)
Evictions	=	502
Total debt	=	£1m
Debt collected	=	£50k

Figure 4: Waste in pursuing tenants to court

The table above (*Figure 4*) shows the waste in our processes of pursuing tenants to court with the goal of evicting them and re-securing the property and the outstanding debt. In getting decrees for 962 tenancies that caused former tenant debt of £1m, we have recovered only £50,000. Actual figures are not available but there is enough evidence to show that a significant number of the families involved eventually re-presented as homeless and entered the system once again. Many others remained in the same house but started a new tenancy (a technical eviction). The end result was the waste of a huge amount of effort, energy and money by the GHA, and cost, frustration and anxiety for the tenants.

Of the 23,000 tenants who were in debt at the start of the year and who triggered the processes for court action, only 962 decrees were granted (15% of the total). To get to that stage involved at least 47,000 activities not counting case conferences, letters and interviews in the local offices. Having secured these decrees, we then only carried out 502 evictions and of the total debt due from these tenants (£1m) we only recovered £50,000 through the court process (*Figure 4*). At least £50,000 would have been expended on the process once staff time and other expenses are taken into account.

So, in short, the exercise of taking tenants to court adds no financial value at all to our business. The wider social costs are also not taken into account. Many of these evicted families re-appear, some presenting as homeless and others emerging again at a later date having stayed with friends and family. We have a spiralling social problem with a huge price tag attached.

Changes to the court criteria

At this stage, we had recognised all the waste that is inherent in the court system, and the detrimental impact this was having on our customers. They saw us doing nothing more than sending out letters, legal notices by the dozen and requiring their engagement in a worthless process that did little to help them with their financial problems. We set about revising our approach to pursuing cases through court.

First, we ensured that our Purpose of collecting rent was uppermost in the minds of staff. All activity was front-loaded to ensure that tenants could financially sustain a tenancy and that we were engaged with them in supporting their actions to keep clear rent accounts. Where it did become necessary to pursue court action, this would only be with the direct and active involvement of the local Housing Manager.

If the seriousness of the situation was demonstrated and a Notice of Proceedings for Recovery of Possession (NPRP) had to be raised, it could only be done with the active involvement and consent of the manager following a series of rigorous reviews. Prior to this we were producing over 600 NPRPs per 4-week period (*Figure 5*).

After implementing the changes, we are now averaging 70 NPRPs per 4-week period (a 90% reduction). The validity of such legal action is showing returns – amongst tenants and certainly amongst the Sheriffs.

We are no longer viewed as an organisation which dishes out legal notices in the expectation that the Sheriffs will do our work for us and no longer do we need two sittings per week for Sheriffs to hear all our cases. In fact we can demonstrate financial savings across the board as a result of the reviews.

Whilst much of our emphasis has been on new tenants, we are also working with existing tenants in arrears and supporting them to pay their rent whilst clearing backlogged debt. By the end of the financial year 2008/09 our total arrears debt had decreased from £10.1m to £7.99m reflecting a greater number of tenants maintaining a more stable payment pattern.

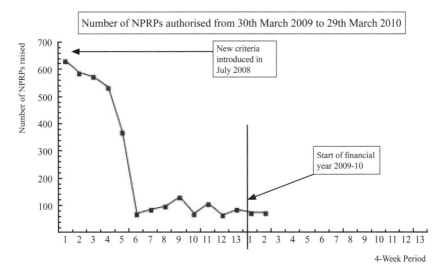

Figure 5: Notice of Proceedings for Recovery of Possession (NPRP) decline

Having designed and tested the solutions and having rolled some out directly (e.g. the new court criteria via a briefing to the Managers' Assembly supported by information packs, a dedicated website and one-to-one support), the Business Improvement Leaders (BIL) group then re-formed.

In September 2008 the BIL group was expanded to ten. They took an intensive three week programme to become fully accredited Vanguard Consultants. They then worked their way around Glasgow introducing systems thinking firstly to local managers and then to their teams. They shared with them the pain of checking Purpose, gathering demand data and analysing the results. They helped staff build systems pictures and discover how wide of perfect their office was. Then they trained and supported staff to ensure that they all understood 'Perfect', and knew why our processes had to change. Staff and managers started looking at the business through a fresh pair of customer's eyes.

Systems thinking produces results when managers change their thinking about the business. Managers only truly understand their customers' demands when they 'walk the walk', following the process from end to end. This then guides them in how to change the process to better meet those demands. To engage staff fully in the process we have introduced a highly visual tool, the Visual Measures Board (VMB). The board is usually mobile, double sided and rotating. It allows managers to display pictorially the results of the demand analysis, the top three failure demands, some key measures, and critical hassles for staff.

With the team, the manager is then able to discuss and agree a possible solution, or experiment, that should result in improved performance or reduction in failure. Period on period monitoring will hopefully demonstrate the success of the experiment. If it doesn't, the team can reconsider and design another experiment and again watch for improvement. Each period the measures charts are refreshed. An example of this would be the end-to-end time from a new tenant moving in to a house, to first payment being made (*Figure 6*). We've refined the charts so that we can also distinguish between those tenants who pay direct and those who receive housing benefit to pay their rent.

Our goal with these charts is to identify the causes of variation and to develop a solution that will not only improve the performance, but will reduce variation. This is to ensure a consistency of high quality approaches in all our offices.

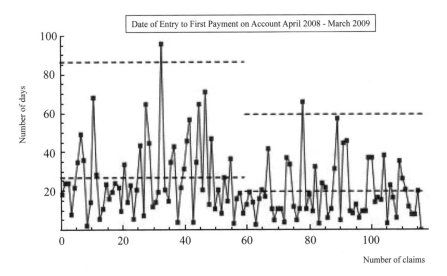

Date of Entry to First Payment on Account April 2008 - March 2009

Figure 6: Time for tenants' first rent payment (dropped from 24 to 17 days in 3 months)

Our team of internal consultants were in turn able to accredit front line managers to practitioner level – a process that continues even now.

Another example of changing process

Another example we identified was in relation to the payment of home loss and/or disturbance when tenants are re-housed in a clearance (i.e. their buildings are to be demolished and we are obliged to give them a new tenancy with statutory compensation). We identified a 17-step process that is still in operation, including the same piece of paper travelling at least 4 times in a GHA mail van between offices in order that different employees can each do one thing with it. The end result is a cheque posted to the host office and a requirement for the tenant to return to that office and sign for it with a further three days wait for the money to clear in their account.

A proposed streamlined solution does away with cheques and more than halves the number of steps required, resulting in a faster and more effective system with secure payment to the tenant.

Common System, Common Sense – the people perspective

Managers within Glasgow Housing Association received a very strong wake up call from the systems thinking intervention in their offices. These three examples show how their thinking has changed:

i). Carolyn Lennon, Community Housing Manager

> *'Looking at the way we conduct our business from an end-to-end process and creating a systems picture really opened my eyes up to the waste we make for ourselves. It was also amazing how easy it was to identify the waste and put practices into place to eliminate it. That was my light-bulb moment, i.e. why did it take this intervention to realise what waste we had in our systems!*

> *'Since the intervention I have a "systems picture" head on all the time and I look at all things in an end-to-end way and try to eliminate waste as a natural way of working now. We have always been driven by targets and although we still have contractual targets (homeless, temporary furnished flats (TFFs) etc.) in place, I try to get the message across that it's how we do things and how we can do things better that is more meaningful to me. Working this way should see a natural improvement in performance rather than the usual "targets drive behaviour" way of working.*

> *'The role of my front line workers has changed also. Through the fortnightly Visual Methods Board (VMB) meetings which have been in place since November 08, they have a clear picture of how I want them to think about things and do things differently. This has helped in several parts of our business such as completing a Housing Application Form (HAF) through to the new tenant visit. We eliminated a lot of waste from this end-to-end process and as a result we have seen the number of days from Notice of Termination of the Tenancy (NTT) to Date of Entry (DOE) reducing. Obviously we still have cases which show spikes in our charts but we look at these, find out what's happened and learn from them. The same goes for getting the first payment into the account. We again have improved in this area and learnt from cases where it took longer than others.*

> *'It really is just about adopting common sense!!'*

ii). Michael Ratcliffe, Manager, Glasgow South West was highly sceptical:

> '*During the intervention I was initially a bit suspicious and more than a bit annoyed that my management methods and performance were being challenged! I remained in this frame of mind up to the point when I personally conducted an experiment.*
>
> '*My light bulb moments were around thinking that some things had not changed for 20 years! And what about the duplication! It taught me that I need to look at processes more and examine how to use resources to our best advantage.*
>
> '*I am more involved in the operational/process side of the business than I was before. I used to think of myself as the Orchestra Conductor. Now I know that as well as this I need to regularly pick up an instrument and check that it works!*
>
> '*Everyone is involved in the Visual Methods Board (VMB) fortnightly meetings. Experiments are discussed and issues raised. We try to conduct an experiment every couple of periods and describe to the team the results. We are pleased with the reduction in "Selection to Reselection" times and believe that this has arisen simply by checking if a customer is interested in an offer rather than going through the whole select/offer/ viewing process only to have the house refused two days after the viewing. I now cannot believe we ever followed such a habit-driven process in the past.*
>
> '*We are about to embark on a repeat of the Demand study we carried out in the early days of Common System, Common Sense to examine what has changed. Unfortunately, other than improved performance, we have not yet gathered real evidence of increased customer satisfaction apart from comments from our Committee and being granted Investors in People (IIP) accreditation on 17th April 2009.*'

iii) Joe Lambie & Catherine Athmani, Managers, South Glasgow

> *Joe and Catherine realised they shared some common difficulties in the way rent payments were being handled in their offices, highlighted through the demand analysis and the*

building of a systems picture. The two took a step back from the current work flows, and developed a spreadsheet documenting the way they would both like the rent collection activity to be carried out. This draft is now currently being reviewed by their peer managers. As Joe pointed out: 'It is more important now to manage the process rather than the staff.'

These three examples illustrate that there has been a change in the way the front line managers within GHA are thinking and managing. Interestingly they also report that staff members are acting differently. The Business Improvement Leaders (BILs) who carried out the intervention saw this change too over the three week period, as staff moved from scepticism and wariness to a position of acceptance and recognition that they once again had a voice in suggesting better ways of serving the customer.

Corporate Interventions

Having formed the front-line service teams, the BILs were by the end of May 2009 in a position to carry out interventions with corporate teams. At the time of writing, one intervention has been completed and two more are part-way through. IT was the team that completed an intervention. HR and Welfare Benefits are both progressing positively.

IT Managers followed a similar three week programme to the Local Housing Office (LHO) intervention but spent a good deal of the third week designing 'systems perfect' for some of their processes. This worked particularly well because of the willing engagement of staff from all quarters of the team. Indeed, after the intervention, the multi-functional groups have continued working through the changes and managing experiments for improvement. It is also interesting to observe the quick up-front leadership by staff on these teams, allowing managers to provide support and to remove obstacles to facilitate changes. Further corporate team interventions are being planned for the rest of this financial year.

Achievements 2007/08 v. 2008/09

These are just a few of our significant headlines comparing our position at the end of the financial year 2007/08 to the end of 2008/09:

- Rent arrears down from £10.1m to £7.99m.

- Lettable empty properties rate reduced from 1.4% to 1.27%.

- End-to-end re-let time down 13 days from 56 to 43 days.

- Process of removing non lettables has dropped to 27 days.

- Letting performance is the best since the inception of GHA – lets within 4 weeks rose 18% from 49% to 67%.

There is a long way to go and much still to be done, but the building blocks are now in place across all front line offices. This will allow staff to process customer enquiries in a significantly different way and further improve performance as a consequence.

Conclusions and learning to date

Much of what we have been designing has been with the purpose of ensuring consistency across all business areas so that all customers get the right service in the right place at the right time: *Common System*. We have also recognised that the staff have been trying to apply sensible workable methods only to be frustrated by complicated and convoluted managerial activity. So we are returning to: *Common Sense*. GHA has therefore branded its approach to systems thinking internally as *Common System, Common Sense*.

It was apparent that we were in a circle of complacency before the Regulator's report in September 2007. We believed that our performance was about as good as it could be. We thought we understood our purpose and reasons for existing. We didn't think there was any way to make significant improvement. Our managers generally had 'left' the shop floor and no longer actively listened to their staff.

But after 12 months of systems thinking and 45 interventions in front line local offices the results speak for themselves. We're now rolling out the programme to corporate teams and helping them review the service they provide.

Managers are learning to read and anticipate trends in their own business unit based on weekly actions, experiments and customer demand. They engage directly with the staff through building new systems pictures and allowing staff to suggest and lead on business experiments. Overall, we're leading the field in a number of measures in our benchmarking clubs.

The Business Improvement Leaders have a programme of revisits to all the local offices to support the ongoing performance improvement, to ensure that new colleagues understand the method and to help managers focus on what makes the work work.

The biggest challenge in this second year (2009/2010) is to maintain the success and secure further performance improvements. We need to consolidate the implementation of systems thinking at the front line. We need to quickly help our partners and our other corporate teams to understand and apply systems thinking. This will enable us to enhance our customers' whole end-to-end experience of our service.

About the author

 Graeme Hamilton is a Service Development Manager with Glasgow Housing Association. He has worked in the public housing sector in Glasgow for 24 years. He often engages directly with tenants on the issues that concern them most: applying for and sustaining a tenancy, being able to afford and pay their rent, and resolving concerns with anti-social neighbours.

Graeme has also been an internal Organisational Development adviser and consultant, supporting staff to help their customers in a better way. Graeme has an MSc in Human Resource Management from Glasgow Caledonian University. Along with colleagues, he facilitates the application of systems thinking throughout the Glasgow Housing Association.

Glasgow Housing Association, Granite House, 177 Trongate, Glasgow G1 5HF

Tel: 0141 274 6371   Email: Graeme.hamilton@gha.org.uk

www.gha.org.uk

BIBLIOGRAPHY

Ackoff, Russell L., *The Art of Problem Solving*, John Wiley & Sons, New York, 1987
(Entertaining examples of the power of systems thinking.)

Deming, W. Edwards, *Out of the Crisis*, The MIT Press, Cambridge, Massachusetts, 2000 (A key work on applying Statistical Process Control to management and the remarkable insights this can provide.)

Egan, Gerard, *The Skilled Helper: A Problem-Management Approach to Helping*, Brooks / Cole Publishing, Pacific Grove, California, 6th ed., 1998
(Professional framework and examples on how to help people change.)

Ohno, Taiichi, *Toyota Production System: Beyond Large-Scale Production*, Productivity Press, Cambridge, Massachusetts, 1992
(Seminal book that showed how to transform the organisation of work.)

Scholtes, Peter R., *The Leader's Handbook: Making Things Happen, Getting Things Done*, McGraw-Hill, New York, 1998
(Classic on systems thinking, but tends to treat change as a project rather than integral to an adaptive organisation.)

Schonberger, Richard J., *Japanese Manufacturing Techniques: Nine Hidden Lessons in Simplicity*, The Free Press, New York, 1982
(Fascinating techniques and ideas on how work should be organised to improve quality and reduce costs.)

Seddon, John, *Freedom from Command and Control: a better way to make the work work*, Vanguard Education, Buckingham, 2nd ed., 2005
(Integrates the powerful ideas from Toyota and Deming with change theory to show how to transform service organisations.)

Seddon, John, *Systems Thinking in the Public Sector: the failure of the reform regime and a manifesto for a better way*, Triarchy Press, Axminster, 2008
(Details and examples of how the public sector can improve service while cutting costs.)

Senge, Peter M., *The Fifth Discipline: The Art and Practice of the Learning Organisation*, Random House, London, 1990
(Focus on how systems thinking enables a learning organisation, but implementation method weak.)

Shingo, Shigeo, *A Study of the Toyota Production System*, Productivity Press, Portland, Oregon, 1989
(How to reduce waste in an organisation.)

Taguchi, Genichi, *Robust Engineering: Learn How to Boost Quality While Reducing Costs & Time to Market,* McGraw-Hill, New York, 2000
(Key idea is that if customer needs are precisely understood and satisfied then high quality service at lower cost will result. This is much more effective than the common practice of working to 'tolerances' or ranges of performance.)

Womack, James P., Jones, Daniel T., & Roos, Daniel, *The Machine That Changed the World: The Story of Lean Production,* HarperCollins, New York, 1991
(Readable MIT study of the global car industry that shows how wasteful practices were perceived as good management in the EC and USA – until Toyota showed otherwise. Standardisation which works in manufacturing is often damaging when applied to the variety inherent in service organisations.)

Wheeler, Donald J., *Understanding Variation: The Key to Managing Chaos*, SPC Press, Knoxville, Tennessee, 1993
(Shows why many management reports are often meaningless and misleading. Managers are therefore unaware that their processes and organisation are, in reality, out of control.)

GLOSSARY

Capability: Measures of performance from the customer's point of view. This may include measures of end-to-end time, on-time performance as required by the customer, and the percentage of customer demands resolved at the first point of contact.

Capability Chart: Significantly more powerful than most management information tools. Records performance over time and analyses the variation in the results. It indicates if a process is in or out of control.

Check: This is the process of creating the knowledge of how an organisation is actually working from a customer's perspective. Key data produced is the amount of failure demand and total end-to-end times to serve customers.

Check team: This is a group of the organisation's employees, from different departments and levels of seniority. Their task is to investigate demand and the organisation's current capability to serve its customers. They report regularly on their progress to senior management.

Clean input: Ensuring all documents to be processed are complete and accurate, before work starts. Extra effort at this stage greatly reduces waste and improves response times.

Command and control: This is the dominant management model in the public sector. It does work but is inherently wasteful. It emphasises a top-down, hierarchical approach with a focus on targets, standards and budgets. See *systems thinking* for comparison.

Demand data: This is split into value and failure demand. The failure demand can be eliminated to cut costs and improve customer service. Value demand analysis enables the main types of true demand to be clearly identified.

Demand, nature of: customer demand is generally much more consistent and predictable than is perceived. Therefore assembling precise data on the real nature of demand is invaluable for designing better processes.

Dirty input: This is input to a system, such as a document, that is not complete or accurate. Allowing such data into a system causes waste and delays. Although it takes extra resource at the entry to 'gate keep' a process, it is vital to work 'clean' to save considerable time and money overall.

Emergent: Instead of targets and plans it is more effective to understand your demand and your current capability to meet it. Then carry out experiments to reduce failure demand and improve your capability. The results will far exceed any targets set. This can be disconcerting for 'command and control' managers at first.

End-to-end time: This is a measure of the total time the service took as experienced by the customer. As conventional metrics are of activity within functional management silos, the total time the customer experiences is often not known. This metric often indicates waste and poor performance levels.

Failure demand: Demand caused by a failure to do something or do something right for the customer. Examples would be complicated forms that customers are unable to fill in correctly or commitments made but not kept which generate wasteful 'chase up' work. Failure demand often makes up 20% – 70% of total demand, so reducing this cuts costs, improves service and raises staff morale.

Flow: Understanding the precise path the work takes through your organisation is vital. Unnecessary specialisation of staff often causes the route the work follows to become convoluted. Tracking the work often reveals unnecessary stages, rework and delays.

Hand-offs: Command and control managers believe that specialised units are more effective. But fragmenting the way work is handled requires it to be passed between the specialists. This transferring is an overhead which causes wasteful rework and reduces job satisfaction. Hand-offs are therefore to be kept to a minimum.

Intervention: Engaging with an organisation to help it to improve its performance. The task is to help people learn to see their work differently so they can be more effective managers.

Make normal: Once the work has been understood and the necessary changes made, it takes time for the new processes to become embedded and routine. At this time the organisation may revert to its previous habits, so attention is required to avoid this.

Management – role of: In 'command and control' organisations managers see their role as being to manage people and budgets. In 'systems thinking' their role is to act on the system, to enable their self-managing staff to continually improve how they do their work.

Measures: In 'command and control' organisations measures are top down and focus on budgets, targets and standards. In 'systems thinking' they are integrated with the work and focus on capability and variation. They are empowering for the workforce rather than a mechanism for control and compliance. A key distinction is that the 'command and control' measures are typically arbitrary; systems measures are always real.

Method: this refers to the Vanguard Method for analysing organisations and then intervening to improve their performance. It is based on the work of Deming and Toyota. It emphasises seeing an organisation as a system from a customer's outside perspective rather than top down as a group of functional hierarchies.

Nominal Value: Taguchi's observation that by first understanding exactly what a customer wants we can then aim at perfection. This is significantly better than working to tolerances or a range of performance.

People problem: Command and control with its contractual approach and reliance on extrinsic motivation often experiences high staff sickness absence and labour turnover. This is then perceived as a 'people problem' and responded to, often ineffectively, with more rules and regulations. It is a 'normal' result of this approach to management. Systems thinking with its emphasis on intrinsic satisfaction and learning has a more positive work environment and therefore fewer staff issues.

Predictable demand: demand is usually remarkably consistent. By capturing the data to demonstrate this, process redesign is made much simpler and more effective.

Preventable demand: This is another term for failure demand that may be more acceptable and easier for an organisation to adopt. Important to note that only predictable failure demand is preventable. Unexpected outliers mean that things will still go wrong, but the large numbers of routine failures can be eliminated.

Purpose: This must be defined in customer terms for a coherent and aligned organisation. Commonly organisations work to a *de facto* purpose such as 'make the budget' or 'achieve the activity target'. This is dysfunctional as peoples' efforts and ingenuity become focused on 'the plan' rather than the customer.

Rechecking: If an organisation is split into many specialist, functional units, then each time the work is passed between the units, it is usually 'rechecked'. This duplication is wasteful and does not add value to the customer.

Redesign phase: Once the purpose, profile of demand and the true capability of the organisation to service this demand have been understood, then experiments can take place to work out how to improve. The organisation can then be redesigned using this new knowledge.

Rework: If a process is fragmented then oversight can be lost and different stages will inadvertently make work for, and inflict costs on, each other. This is common where organisations are sub-optimised into specialist functional units.

Roll-in: A method to scale up a change to the whole organisation that was successful in one unit. Change is not imposed. Instead each area needs to learn how to do the analysis of waste for themselves and devise their own solutions. This approach engages the workforce and produces better, more sustainable solutions. Compare to 'roll-out'.

Roll-out: Method that involves developing an improved process, standardising it and applying it to other areas. This tends to create two problems: first, the solution is not optimised for each specific context so is not a good fit; secondly, the staff in the other units have not been through the same learning and therefore feel little sense of ownership. They may also feel a loss of control and resist change.

Root causes: The Toyota process of the '5 whys?' is used to get to the real source of a problem by asking 'why?' five times. Attention is focused on finding and fixing the source of a problem rather than its symptoms.

Scope / Scoping: The practice of defining the part of an organisation to be analysed and improved. Too large and the resources available for change will be ineffective; too small and significant results will not be achieved.

Silo: The practice of organising workers into separate functional hierarchies. Each silo tends to work to optimise their own performance, but the result is a damaging sub-optimisation overall. This can be measured by recording the total end-to-end time experienced by customers to receive a service.

System conditions: The causes of waste. These are the measures, targets or rewards that influence how a system performs. Others include: I.T. systems, management behaviour, organisational structures, rules and procedures. Understanding these is critical. For example, a target that all emails must be replied to within 24 hours may well result in busy people sending 'random' replies to meet the target. Unless this system condition is removed, and the underlying issues addressed, limited improvement will be possible. The vital point is that you need to understand the key system conditions in any particular flow.

System design: Once the purpose of the organisation is clear from a customer's perspective, and the profile of demand is understood, then the system can be designed to meet this.

Systems thinking: The process starts from seeing the whole from a customer's perspective and recognising the inter-dependence of the parts. Then it works outside in from a customer's perspective. The key is to design the system against known patterns of demand. The role of management is to act on the system. Data is empowering and shared to allow staff to learn and self-organise.

Targets: These are often arbitrary and not based on knowledge. For example: 'we need a 3% cost saving'. But if the pattern of demand, current capability to meet this demand and the flow of work are known, usually far bigger savings are achievable with improved performance.

Traditional management thinking: A 'command and control' mindset, which believes a top down hierarchy with a functional organisational design is the only way to manage. There is an emphasis on control, extrinsic motivation of staff and contractual relationships.

Unclean input: see dirty input.

Value demand: This is demand that you do want. This comes from customers who are requesting new services and updating their accounts. It is the reason the organisation exists.

Vanguard Method: Focuses on how to analyse and design work, and then how to make the change to a better performing organisation. See Method. It is emergent, meaning that it is concerned with establishing the profile of customer demand and the organisation's capability to meet it. From this solid foundation experiments can be made to improve performance. This is quite different from trying to obtain results by ensuring compliance to arbitrary targets and basing plans on opinion not knowledge.

Variance: There are natural fluctuations in all processes. They will not perform uniformly all the time. Variation is the random and miscellaneous component that undermines simple and limited comparisons. To see the 'voice of the process' data must be presented in time series to establish if it is under control.

Waste: Any activity that does not add value to the customer.

About Triarchy Press

Triarchy Press is an independent publishing house that looks at how organisations work and how to make them work better. We present challenging perspectives on organisations in short and pithy, but rigorously argued, books.

Other titles in the areas of Systems Thinking and organisational learning include:

> *Systems Thinking in the Public Sector* by John Seddon
>
> *Systems Thinking for Curious Managers* by Russell Ackoff with Herbert Addison and Andrew Carey
>
> *Management f-Laws* by Russell Ackoff, Herbert Addison and Sally Bibb
>
> *The Search for Leadership* by William Tate
>
> *The Organisational Leadership Toolkit* by William Tate
>
> *Adventures in Complexity* by Lesley Kuhn
>
> *Organising and Disorganising* by Michael Thompson.

Through our books, pamphlets and website we aim to stimulate ideas by encouraging real debate about organisations in partnership with people who work in them, research them or just like to think about them.

Please tell us what you think about the ideas in this book at:

> www.triarchypress.com/telluswhatyouthink

If you feel inspired to write – or have already written – an article, a pamphlet or a book on any aspect of organisational theory or practice, we'd like to hear from you. Submit a proposal at:

> www.triarchypress.com/writeforus

For more information about Triarchy Press, or to order any of our publications, please visit our website or drop us a line:

> www.triarchypress.com

We're now on Twitter: @TriarchyPress
and Facebook: www.facebook.com/triarchypress

About John Seddon

John Seddon trained as an occupational psychologist and is known around the world for his pioneering work on change in public and private sector organisations. He translated and adapted the Toyota Production System (TPS) for use by service organisations.

He is also known as an informed and controversial critic of management fads and much of the theory that has underpinned public sector reform. He is a leading advocate of Systems Thinking in business and the public sector and a widely published author who lectures at seminars, conferences and universities around the world.

He is Managing Director of Vanguard Ltd, a consultancy specialising in organisational change, a Visiting Professor at Cardiff and Derby Universities and a fellow of the public policy think-tank ResPublica.

He can be contacted at: office@vanguardconsult.co.uk

About Dr Peter Middleton

Senior Lecturer at Queen's University Belfast, Peter is an acknowledged specialist in service and software quality. Winner of the North American Shingo Prize for Applied Research Excellence in 2007, he has worked with organisations like:

Hewlett-Packard, Northrop Grumman, Software Productivity Consortium, IBM, Tata Information Systems and the Delta Institute, Copenhagen.

He can be contacted at: p.middleton@qub.ac.uk

In Praise of *Delivering Public Services that Work*:

"The WLGA sees the work of John Seddon as essential to public services reform and achieving a systems overhaul to transform delivery to the benefit our communities. The case studies in this volume are further evidence of the impact of systems theory on front line services particularly within local government and the need to liberate managers from pointless edicts and targets which litter the public sector. I have been hugely impressed with the impact that the work of John and his colleagues has had in challenging traditional thinking and shifting public services to design against demand. In turn it produces the wonderful outcome that managers abandon the pursuit of meeting redundant indicators and concentrate on public expectations for better services."
Steve Thomas, Chief Executive, Welsh Local Government Association (WLGA)

"This book provides any leader charged with service performance improvement and simultaneous cost reduction all the information necessary to deliver real-world improvement to customers. This method is well proven in my own organisation."
Dr Carlton Brand, Corporate Director, Resources – Wiltshire Council

"Everyone involved in the delivery of public services on the ground should understand the principles that underpin systems thinking. John Seddon has become a one man army in his battle to dismantle today's command state and inspection industry. These case studies show how the application of the Vanguard method transforms the lives of both the customers and the people who deliver our local public services. This is essential reading for anyone who is interested in delivering better local services at lower cost."
Stephen Greenhalgh, Leader, Hammersmith & Fulham Council and Head of the Conservative Councils Innovation Unit

"The systems thinking approach that has been developed by John Seddon gives powerful insights into the way that organisations work. The common sense approach immediately engages those who are working in the system and is easily understood by those who are taken through the process. This book shows that the approach is relevant to any organisation providing a service. It gives valuable demonstrations of the difficulties in adopting a new approach, and of the advantages to be gained by doing so."
Adrian R. Bull, Chief Executive, Queen Victoria Hospital, Sussex